Stranded in Skin and Bones

STRANDED in SKIN and BONES

Faith
Within
the Madness

Robert Stofel

RESOURCE *Publications* • Eugene, Oregon

STRANDED IN SKIN AND BONES
Faith Within the Madness

Copyright © 2020 Robert Stofel. All rights reserved. Except for brief quotations in critical publications or reviews, no part of this book may be reproduced in any manner without prior written permission from the publisher. Write: Permissions, Wipf and Stock Publishers, 199 W. 8th Ave., Suite 3, Eugene, OR 97401.

Resource Publications
An Imprint of Wipf and Stock Publishers
199 W. 8th Ave., Suite 3
Eugene, OR 97401

www.wipfandstock.com

PAPERBACK ISBN: 978-1-5326-9719-7
HARDCOVER ISBN: 978-1-5326-9720-3
EBOOK ISBN: 978-1-5326-9721-0

Manufactured in the U.S.A.   JUNE 4, 2020

Grateful Acknowledgment is made for the original publication of the following essays, some of which appear here with a few changes: "The Role of Fiction in Suicidal Ideations," *Brevity;* "*The Lost, the Damned, the Forgotten,*" Anderbo; "*Leaving the Cow-House,*" Harpur Palate; "*A Place for People Like Us,*" Bare Root Review; "*Dispatches from Lala Land,*" Red Clay Review; "The Secret Lives of Cows," Passages North.

This book is lovingly dedicated to the memory of
Patti Whitehurst

Son, your little face is pitiful. Son, we can't just let you roam the streets like some kind of crazy animal. Son, you got to get your natural impulses curbed. You've got to get your corners knocked off, son you got to get realistic.

—DONALD BARTHELME, *THE DEAD FATHER*

Contents

Introduction | ix

Leppy | 1
J.B. Cook Auto Parts | 5
Citizen's Arrest | 10
The Farm | 15
Coconut | 29
Making Hay | 39
Brentwood Girls | 44
Wide Awake | 47
The Phone Number | 48
Brown Sugar | 51
The Front Gate | 58
Rescuing a Horse | 62
The Town Square | 65
The Bottom of the Bottle | 71
The Probability of a Pierced Heart | 75
A Longing for Hope | 78
Graduation | 81
Clippings | 82
Back in the Saddle | 85

Mr. Gatti's | 88
Eleven | 91
Pumping Gas | 94
Set Free | 96
Demoniac | 98
Let Me Introduce You | 101
The Basement | 103
The Lord's Chapel | 106
Hefty | 111
The Dumpster Man | 115
Gone in 60 Seconds | 118
Brand New | 122
Fifty Dollar Man | 124
Father and Son | 127
Valentine's Day | 131
Tuesday Bible Study | 132
The Drug Dealer and the Gun | 135
Reba's Trees | 138
Remission | 140
Mass-a-two-setts | 143
Freddy's Coming for You | 147
Gone | 150
On the Road | 151
Music Therapy | 154
Endnotes | 162
Bibliography | 165

Introduction

Life is suffering in skin and bones. There is no way out of this body. No holes of escape. No lagoons of nirvana where we can wash away the stain. No route for the blood but round and round. Sure, we can bleed. We can bleed until death. Then the soul will go somewhere. But who wants to bleed? Who knows where the soul really goes? We have our beliefs. Different philosophies abound about how we are rescued from this bag of skin and bones. Because there are two sides of the soul—the broken side and the redeemed one. We cannot separate them. Not here. Not in this place. So the choice comes to everyone—God or money? Darkness or light? Peace or madness? This is our dilemma. We are stranded in skin and bones. Here with the animals.

Leppy

Joseph A. Munk said: *If a calf loses its mother while very young it is called a "leppy." Such an orphan calf is, indeed, a forlorn and forsaken little creature. Having no one to care for it, it has a hard time to make a living. If it is smart enough to share that lacteal ration of some more fortunate calf it does very well, but if it cannot do so and has to depend entirely on grazing for a living its life becomes precarious and is apt to be sacrificed in "the struggle for the survival of the fittest."*[1]

1974

Carl, my father's friend, knocked on the door three nights after my mother secretly moved out. I was watching television from a lawn chair that I'd retrieved from the backyard and placed in the living room.

My father said to Carl, "Hang on. We're just about ready."

I nodded at Carl standing in the door.

He nodded back and rocked on the balls of his feet. He had a rawboned face with a cigarette hanging from his lip. His shoes were greasy. Most of my father's friends wore greasy shoes. He had bushy eyebrows and kept the eye above the cigarette squinted to keep the smoke out as he leaned in the doorway and looked at me with the other eye.

My father reentered the room with my shoes and dropped them beside the chair. "Put these on. We're going somewhere."

I didn't ask why or where we were going. It was that kind of day.

That morning I'd walked four blocks to my middle school and returned to find the furniture gone, my mother gone, my father on our mustard-colored wall phone with the cord stretched as far as it would go, begging my mother to come home. I gazed around at the empty walls and rooms. I had no idea she wanted to leave us. He glanced at me and I mouthed—"What happened?" But he turned away and said, repeatedly into the phone, "I love you. Why don't you come back home?"

It was the first time I'd ever heard him say he loved her.

My mother came from poverty. Rural Tennessee and nine siblings. Three of my uncles died under suspicious circumstances. One died in a hunting accident. One in a single car accident. Another died from a shotgun blast to the stomach. They found him with his shoe off. Supposedly he used his toes to pull the trigger. Police declared it a suicide. My mother said he was murdered. But only God knows for sure. She knew pain and loss. Pregnant by the age of seventeen. She married my father and went to work in a factory where she fell in love with her supervisor. Somewhere in the process of manufacturing Christmas wrapping paper at the factory—surrounded by the daily spirit of Christmas—she flirted with upward mobility and won her supervisor's affection. He had money and drove a Corvette. He lived in an upscale apartment complex across the street from the high school. My father couldn't compete with the supervisor. He had what my father couldn't afford—means to a larger house and a new car. Soon she became a suburban tennis wife.

Before Carl arrived, I'd helped my father design new living room furniture. We built tables out of boxes we retrieved from the corner store's dumpster. We replaced the chairs covered with 1776 Revolutionary War fabric—drummer boys and soldiers holding rifles—with lawn chairs. As we placed a black and white television on top of a stack of boxes, my father said, "Son, I did everything I could do. I'm sorry."

This was his opening argument.

Carl would deliver the closing remarks.

Outside in the driveway, Carl said, "We gonna teach you a lesson about women." Carl swung open the door of his Pontiac GTO. It let out a metallic squeal. "Get your skinny-self in there."

I slid across the seat, pitching a few beer cans in the floorboard, trying to make some room. Carl got behind the wheel and turned up the country music station out of Nashville. He tapped his fingers to the beat of the song on top of the steering wheel and backed out of the driveway.

Uncertainty was in the air along with bitterness. I didn't say anything. I was content to ride. They drank whiskey, passing it back and forth like two teenage boys. My father cringed as he swallowed. His Adam's apple jutted out against squalid skin. The old car labored under the weight of Carl's foot on the gas. Nobody said a word. Just George Jones singing.

Their silence scared me. Carl was never silent. The man could talk your ears off about nothing. Rattle on about how many deer he killed last year, rattle on about what he'd do if he had money. But he was mute. No rattling. Just the tapping. He threw the cigarette out the window.

We cruised past Sonic, past Piggly-Wiggly, past Wendy's on the left. Making our way to the outskirts of Franklin, Tennessee where the high school emerged. Carl made a left-hand turn into an apartment complex. George Jones gave way to Johnny Cash. His baritone growl forced its way into the tension, along with June Carter Cash's sweet voice. Carl downshifted and crept over a speed bump. The car squeaked on its haunches, the tailpipe drug. Carl craned his pointed head to look at me. "We gonna show you what women all about, boy."

I nodded and leaned up to get a better view. I had no idea. The clubhouse came into view on the left. The swimming pool motionless and winterized. I had friends that lived in that apartment complex. During the summer, we performed can-openers and cannonballs off the board, splashing the girls who sunbathed, as residents barbecued on their patios. The smoke rising to the top of the third story apartment complex, and then evaporating over the roofs. But that night all of this was out of season.

Carl backed into a space between two cars, facing an apartment with curtains slightly open in the middle of the plate glass windows. The DJ on the radio was talking about the party they were throwing at the Sheraton. "Brush up on your two-step . . . Bring your partner." The DJ trailed his words off at the end.

I asked, "Why are we sitting here?"

"You'll see," Carl said.

We sat motionless for five minutes. Nobody breathed a word.

A car turned into the section of the parking lot where we sat. My father looked up for the first time. Carl whispered, "Hunker down." We slumped. Carl turned off the radio. I heard a car door slam in the distance. Carl said, "Look, boy. Look up here. There's your mama!"

I peeked through buttery smears on the windshield.

My mother crossed the parking lot in a skimpy blue skirt, I'd never seen her so confident. She knocked, and the door opened. A man's face appeared. He stepped aside to let her in.

My father never spoke. He let Carl do his talking. And Carl said, "Boy, you got to watch women. They'll mess you up every time. Ain't met a woman yet that won't cheat on you."

The buttery smears on the windshield coalesced in my veins.

What George Armatage said: *It may here be remarked that on first leaving the cow-house, the calf should be confined in a safe place in the yard or elsewhere for a day or two, until it becomes accustomed to the bright light of day, as on its first introduction it appears almost blind, and would likely to run into danger.*[2]

J.B. Cook Auto Parts

1975

Most towns are made up of moments. Little chunks of history chained together—decades aligned with years, and years combined with the present moment. Franklin, Tennessee has had its moments. Five tragic hours of a Civil War battle. Six dead Confederate generals. Franklin has a history, but today it's a vibrant community south of Nashville. A Target store sits at the base of a battlefield. Above it on Breezy Hill General Hood sat on his horse with his field glasses overlooking the realization that he faced too many Yankees in the trenches below. But he sent the Army of Tennessee anyway, and they charged a town that will forever be known for that Civil War battle. Those five hours scar the town's history, and the town fathers named six streets after each dead general.

Cleburne Street
Carter Street
Strahl Street
Adams Street
Granbury Street
Gist Street

Stranded in Skin and Bones

Franklin is home to big money now. But in the 1970s and early 1980s it was at best a Cowtown, a sleepy little community, and my father owned an auto parts store downtown during this era. The square brick edifice with two large plate-glass windows across the front was where my father stood behind the counter in a blue uniform shirt that had *J.B. Cook Auto Parts* over one pocket and *Billy* over the other. A pegboard lined with screwdrivers and wrenches hung as a backdrop behind the counter. Most everything was behind the counter in those days. The clock on the wall clanked above a sign that read: *If you don't think the dead rise, then you should be around here at quitting time.*

We believed in the American Dream and American cars were a part of that dream. Our heroes were circling the high banks of Talladega and Daytona. And the eagle flied on Friday at my father's auto parts store. But it all changed when the foreign car influence made it harder for the shade-tree mechanic to work on them. Back then anyone with the God-given talent to fix things could turn a wrench and make a buck. All of that is gone now. Gone are the muscle cars, gone are the shade-tree mechanics, gone are the mom and pop auto parts stores. Emissions control systems and internet capabilities carry the day. But there was once a world where the auto parts store was the hub that kept cars and trucks moving around Franklin. My father spent ten hours a day behind the counter waiting on mechanics to walk in and hand him a greasy auto part in a blue shop rag along with the message, "Got one of these?" He'd peel the shop rag away from the old used part like a surgeon laying open flesh to reveal cancer. Take one look. Then walk back an aisle and retrieve the correct part. He knew the business.

My father employed a quirky bunch of employees at the auto parts store, who were nicknamed Time Bomb, Badfinger, Bunt, Nap, and Coma. Mostly high school dropouts with basic car knowledge. And the highlight of my day was when one of these tatted boys—before tattoos were cool—would pick me up after school in one of my father's delivery trucks, and I'd spend my afternoons at the store, watching them so I could emulate them and dress like them—blue jeans and concert T-shirts.

J.B. Cook Auto Parts

It snowed early the year my mother left my father and me. It collected on the flat roof of the auto parts store and turned the streets into slippery slopes for Chryslers, Chevrolets and Fords, and the more it snowed, the more wiper blades stuck to frozen windshields. Then radiators cracked and thermostats failed, causing heaters to blow only cold air. Cars and trucks were in a crisis. The deep freeze had the phones ringing off the hook while salt trucks peppered the front windows of the store with each pass on their way to the main throughways. But business eventually ground to a halt due to the amount of snow accumulation and mechanics gathered at my father's store. Back then, the local auto parts store was like the old country store where people just hung around to socialize. Sometimes they arm-wrestled on the counter. And that day they traversed the storm and found their way to my father's store, where they stabbed the counter with their greasy elbows and locked hands for another ultimate arm-wrestling contest. Someone would yell go and all manners of sounds would emit from the wrestlers. Some groaned, while others yelled out obscenities. And money passed hands when men were defeated, as other men won. And that day, I could feel us breaking away from the icy streets that imprisoned us. Like an iceberg floating in a primordial soup, evolving with every cheer that erupted in a communal gladness we rarely experienced. A tectonic shift in the plates.

Then in walked a guy we all called the Swede. He was a giant—6'6," blonde hair, blue eyes. Arms like the Incredible Hulk. He ate raw hamburger meat for lunch and worked in a garage behind the auto parts store that specialized in repairing exotic-foreign cars, which back then consisted of Toyotas and Datsuns, with an occasional Volvo and BMW thrown in.

Before this day, the Swede had been matched with every mechanic and Harley Davidson rider in town. The Swede had beaten all of them—hands down. The brave ones only lasted eight seconds or less. He'd slam his opponents hand down on the counter with so much force their knuckles actually said the word, "Pop!"

But a new challenger had stepped forward to take on the Swede. He was a farm boy, a commoner, a boy with dirt beneath his nails and muck on his shoes. Just a simple lad, whose brother worked for my father at the auto parts store. The farm boy was raised working in cotton fields, hauling hay, and chopping tobacco.

The farm boy got on one side of the counter, the Swede on the other, while Time Bomb—who had been banned from school property for calling in a bomb threat—took all the phones off the hook, so no one would call and interrupt the action. And once the farm boy held his own for eight seconds with the Swede bearing down on his wrist in ways we'd never seen the Swede bear down before, we realized the farm boy might have a chance.

It was the first time we'd ever seen the Swede grimace. At twenty seconds their wrists hadn't budged. We started looking at each other, like, "What? The Farm Boy? Could he really beat the Swede?"

Then the Swede's wrist buckled back like an open Pez dispenser, and the store fell silent. We'd never seen the Swede's wrist bend backwards even a fraction of an inch. Then his knuckles thumped the counter and the Swede couldn't believe it. He looked at his hand, working it—open, shut, open, shut. Snowflakes like confetti fell outside and accumulated on the roof of the store, while cheers went up and mechanics slapped the farm boy on the back. Later, the farm boy and his brother beat-up a man for messing with his brother's wife. War had been fought in this town before. Mutilated boys. Tod Carter served in the Army of Tennessee during the Battle of Franklin. He had yelled, "I am almost home! Come with me, boys!" Federal troops wounded him near his home while his frightened family huddled in the basement of the now historic Carter House. Nine bullet wounds—a Yankee volley. He lingered through the night and died the next morning in his own bed.

The white picket fence still stands today, along with the two chimneys on each end of the house. On a field trip to the Carter House in the fifth grade, we put our fingers in the bullet holes.

I ran to my father's office. He hadn't even moved from his desk to see about the commotion.

"Dad!" I gasped. "The Swede went down. He was defeated."

J.B. Cook Auto Parts

My father offered a weak smile. Nothing during those days could bring him back to life. All thoughts were on my mother. Around this time—and against my mother's wishes—my father had called my grandparents. Her mother and father arrived at our house, and I can remember it seeming so odd because it was the first time my grandparents had ever visited our house. My father was so sure they would convince their daughter to stay in the marriage. I was told to go outside and play. I threw a ball against the back of the house, knowing something was wrong, but I didn't know for sure. Ten minutes later, while playing in the dirt, I watched my mother climb out the bedroom window and escape. She told them she was going to the bathroom.

"Mom," I yelled after her.

But she slipped away.

Sure, I asked her why she moved out without telling me. She said my father had threatened her life, which has never made sense. Why not take your son? But I gave her the benefit of the doubt. Maybe she was in danger. I'm not sure. And we floated away from there. A child doesn't know the heart of a mother. But I thought the abandonment had something to do with me.

I watched the Swede put on his leather jacket, as Time Bomb said, "Where are you going? The best two out of three. What do you say?"

The Swede waved him off with a chuckle and left. I heard the squeaks of his feet in the snow. The door closed behind him.

The dead came to life that day, long before quitting time. And we floated away from there.

Citizen's Arrest

1974

A month before my mother left us, she had been the subject of a citizen's arrest. My mother had a disagreement with two women over the laws of a stop sign. It centered on who arrived first and who should yield. To the left of us at the four-way, two women pulled up at the same time as my mother and I did. It was a dead heat. A tie. So, according to the laws of the stop sign, who goes first?

The woman's car lunged forward two feet, and then stopped because my mother had done the same. Now she was shocked and stopped the car. Again, it was a face off and she waited for them to yield.

"Don't they know how to drive?" she said, turning down the radio. "You're supposed to stop!" she yelled at them through the front windshield. She shook her finger.

They started across the intersection, but my mother gunned the car and cut them off.

They slammed on the brakes, narrowly missing us. Then they turned and followed us to the next stop sign, blowing their horn and shaking their fingers at us. My mother floored it.

Turning in my seat, I saw the driver's mouth moving, head tilted toward us, and then I saw the other woman with a pen and pad in her hand, writing down our license number.

"They're crazy," my mother cried out.

Then they turned and went in a different direction from us.

Three days after the incident at the stop sign with the two women, a ticket arrived in the mail along with a letter. My mother had been cited by a citizen for running a stop sign. It was a citizen's arrest.

"Whoever heard of such a thing?" my father said later that evening.

"I'm not paying this ticket," my mother said.

I was in the chair across from my father with half of my arm stuck in a Captain Crunch cereal box, looking for the secret prize, watching *Starsky and Hutch*.

"It's your word against theirs," my father said.

"I'm taking Robbie with me."

My father looked my way.

Starsky and Hutch had cornered a guy in a Mustang in a back alley. Hutch jumped out of the Grand Torino and slid across the hood on his way to tackle the bandit that fled. I eased up from the couch, trying to make my own silent getaway to my bedroom. I knew she'd drag me into this mess.

She called after me, "Go get your suit and bring it in here. Let me make sure it still fits. I swear you are growing faster than a weed. Don't look at me like that. Move it!"

My mother and I went to court. I wore the only suit I owned—the suit I wore each time an uncle died suddenly.

The city courthouse sat at the opposite end of the town square. The stop sign at the end of Main Street was where the offense had taken place, and, in a way, we were returning to the scene of the crime. Only this time my mother stopped and looked in all directions before she proceeded to park the car on the side of the street near the courthouse.

The two women were already inside the courtroom. They sat on a wooden bench at the front. They glared at us.

The bailiff called out the docket for the day, and we were slated to go after someone who had been arrested for DUI. I leaned over and asked my mother, "What's a DUI?"

She shooed me away, then placed her plump finger across her lips.

When the bailiff called out my mother's case, I followed her through a swinging wooden gate. We stood in an area where a microphone hung out over a podium. The two women stood beside us.

The judge said, "Do I understand correctly that you, Mrs. Johnson, and you, Mrs. Leech, are here today because y'all filed a citizen's arrest concerning a stop sign violation? Is this correct?"

"Yes, Your Honor," said one of the women. "She ran the stop sign and almost hit us. She was driving recklessly."

The judge said, "I'll have to say, this is unique. Can you tell me exactly what happened?"

The woman swallowed hard. "We were on our way home from the grocery store, and we pulled up to the stop sign, right out here, Your Honor. Right outside the Courthouse." She pointed behind her at the concrete block wall painted the color of seafoam green. She continued, "We pulled up, looked in all directions, then started across, when she just ran the stop sign and almost hit us."

"Is this the way it happened, Mrs. Stofel," the judge said.

"No, Your Honor, not at all."

"Okay, what happened?"

"I got to the stop sign first. Then they pulled up," she said, pointing at them. She gave them her evil-eyed glance and continued, "I sat there a second longer, looked in all directions, then eased out on my way home. Then I heard my son here," she patted my head, "yell out, 'Watch out, Mama!' and they about hit us, Your Honor."

The judge looked at me. His wild eyebrows sprouted over the top of his eyeglasses. He said, "What did you see, son?"

I was terrified. The seafoam green walls rushed at me. A wave broke on the deck of the courtroom and washed over me. Boards creaked. Sails flapped. The building rocked. I hung on for dear life. Afraid to answer. I didn't want to say the wrong thing and ruin the case for my mother, nor did I want to speak against the two women. I knew my mother almost ran them over, so I shrugged my shoulders.

My mother nudged me, but I was a deaf and dumb child.

"Son, can you tell me what happened?" the judge tried again.

I shook my head.

He stared at me a little longer, and then turned to one of the women and asked, "Mrs. Leech, what was so severe about this violation that made you involve the police?"

"Well, other than almost hitting us in the side, we felt her attitude was way out of line and needed to be brought to your attention. She blew her horn and shook her finger at us, Your Honor."

The judge looked down at his bench for a second, and then he looked at my mother. She was pale. She said, "It's the other way around. They shook their finger at me."

"Well, shaking fingers or not, I want you to pay the fine for running a stop sign and court costs. And Mrs. Stofel, I think you owe them an apology." Then before my mother could answer, he banged his gavel and said, "Next case."

I turned into a blob that my mother pulled by the arm, as we pushed through the glass doors and stepped outside. There was no parking lot to speak of, so we had parked on the street. The two women walked on the opposite side of the street. My mother and the two women bantered insults across the street like a tennis match, while I stomped cracks in the sidewalk and followed her to the car.

In the car, she glared at me, but didn't say anything about the courtroom scene. Her face sullen, her shoulders drooped. Then she sped away.

When we pulled into our driveway, I said, "What are you going to tell Daddy?"

She said, "More than you told the judge. Now go to your room."

That night a fight ensued. I heard my father complaining about the court costs and the ticket. "Why did you let them railroad you? You should have fought back. We can't pay this."

"Robbie is the one that didn't standup for me. A cat got his tongue."

My father said, "He's a kid. What did you expect?"

My mother said she'd pay it, and it would be the last thing she'd pay for. She told him not to worry about it. My mother slammed a few doors, while my father called her derogatory names. Both were volatile together when at odds. But mostly my father was distant and overworked. Worrying about a business that would soon be overrun by chain auto parts stores that were making their way to town. Foreign influence crept ever closer. And I think my mother craved more attention, which may have made my father jealous and insecure.

Soon after the citizen's arrest, the supervisor paid movers to move my mother out.

The Farm

2016

Joseph A. Munk said: *A calf when it is hurt is very much like a child, in that it bawls and wants its mamma.*[3]

Rising like heat vapor and rushing toward my pole barn house that sits on a hill. Moving toward me like a herd of awkward buffalo, but they're just simple cows. Red, black, white. Some the color of brown sugar. Laboring by the time they reach the crest of the hill. Flies biting at their backs, their legs, their eyes. It's late afternoon. The setting sun glimmering in puddles of water left from the morning rain. And they've heard my car. They know I'm home. I stand in the driveway knowing it's me they've come to see. But it's not me. They want something a little more than the grass they graze. Something that tastes like molasses. Something the Farmer's CO-OP has concocted and sold to us in a bag labeled "Beef Pellets." High in protein. Plenty of minerals. Like dog treats for cows. They line up at the fence in front of the house and bawl for them.

I imagine them saying, "Come on, man. Where's the pellets? How about a little dessert to go with our grass? That's not too much to ask is it?"

A 50 lb. bag of beef pellets cost about as much as a six-pack of beer. One bag to about 25 cows. Not much. Enough to make their mouths water. We feed the pellets as a supplement, which helps to control them. A pail of pellets can persuade a wayward cow to come home.

The older mama cows push their weight around and get most of the pellets when we pour them in the troughs. They get their noses inside the troughs and push each other back with their heads, repositioning with their backends.

The other day during "pellet time," a young heifer got pushed from behind and landed in the trough on her head. Like she was doing a headstand. Then she fell over on her side. She jumped up and looked at me like, "I'm good. I did that on purpose."

I laughed.

Cows have personalities. Some are shy. Some pushy and bossy. Some are fearful of a rush of wind in the trees or a car horn on the highway. Others chew their cuds with their heads high as royalty. Nothing bothers them. Their calves are always curious. They rush the fence when our dogs come to the barn with us, and then jump wildly if our dogs make a sudden move.

I never thought I'd be working on a farm with my father. It never entered my mind that something like this could happen. But the farm came knocking on our door in the city. My father needed our help. My wife, Jill and I knew nothing about cows before moving to the farm. My father was short of breath and pushing the age of 80. He struggled to maintain the farm and his 50-head of cattle, so we sold our house in Alabama and moved to help him because we thought the farm life sounded refreshing. It sounded so simple, like a step back in time. Homesteaders.

My father had met a widow and married her a few years after my mother divorced him, and he sold his auto parts store and moved to Perry County in West Tennessee to help her on the farm. That was decades ago. Now my stepmother is in her eighties and still able to run her antique store at the edge of the farm, down on Highway 13. She's open Thursday thru Saturday. My father runs the farm. He takes care of the 50-head of beef cattle.

The Buffalo River snakes along the bottom of the farm. Sometimes the cows go swimming. Much to our chagrin. They cross the river and spread out in the green grass of the Buffalo

River Resort on the other side. For the grass is always greener over there. And you wouldn't think they could swim. But those large bodies and small hoofs can fool you. I've watched them get washed downstream, only to find their footing. My heart racing for them, I yelled, "Swim!" Because I was the one who had driven them back across the river to our farm.

    We grow our hay along the banks of the Buffalo River. The water is clear, the stream swift in places. It's the longest unimpounded river in Middle Tennessee. High rock cliffs and an abundance of wildlife in the area. The sign on Highway 13 that welcomes you to Perry County has a tagline that always makes us chuckle: *It's just our nature.* And it's true in some ways. That's the reason rich folk out of Nashville have hunting camps here. Each weekend they rush down Highway 13 pulling their off-road vehicles on trailers with their dually trucks. So, it's true. The only reason you would want to visit a town without a red light and a major grocery store is for the wildlife. The area is depressed when compared to the rest of the state. The economy depends on tourism. And the Buffalo River Resort furnishes us with noise and excitement. Across the river from the farm, campers can canoe, kayak and swim. Camping spots cost $50.00 a night.

    Our first week on the farm, my father had a fainting spell and hit the red dirt road behind his truck, landing beneath the open tailgate. My stepmother helped revive him and rushed him to the hospital in Dickson. Later, he called to tell me I'd have to feed the cows because they were keeping him overnight for observation.

    I panicked. I'd never driven a tractor. To that point, I'd only opened and closed gates for my father, as he drove the tractor. But Jill and I made our way to the haybarn. Two inches of snow covered the ground. The wind out of the north at fifteen miles an hour. A blast of cold, artic air streamed through the region.

    The tractor was inside the haybarn. I hopped into the cab. Pushed in the clutch. Turned the key. Nothing. Not even a click. I tried again and kept trying until Jill told me to Google-it, so I did. We watched a couple of videos, but nothing resembled our tractor.

I kept trying different gear combinations, pushed unknown buttons, flipped a few toggle switches. Nothing.

I said, "The battery must be dead."

Jill said, "Put it in neutral and try it."

It fired right up.

She shot me a wide grin.

Next, I had to learn how to use the needle on the front to stab the huge, round bales of hay and carry them out to the field. Jill smiled and opened the gate to the pasture, while the cows kept their distance, unlike their behavior when my father was at the wheel. Somehow, they sensed our incompetency. They chewed their cuds like old men chewing tobacco on the porch of a country store, watching the city slicker maneuver the tractor. I dropped the large roll of hay in a silver ring that's supposed to save the farmer's hay because the cows can't spread it on the ground.

The cows watched as I tried to back away from the ring. I couldn't. The snow held me there, like quicksand. And I spun the wheels. I worked the clutch. Gave it more gas. Spinning and spitting out mud and snow like the cartoon I'd become. I felt people staring from Highway 13, a two-lane county road that runs along the eastside of the farm. It crosses I-40, in-between Memphis and Nashville. Loretta Lynn's Dude Ranch is on Highway 13. Our farm is south of there.

Some know us as Bill's son and daughter-in-law who moved to Lobelville to help him on the farm. Most don't care. But I wanted to be known as the honorable son who rode into town on a white horse to take care of family. Now I was the one stuck in the field, and unless I got it out, there would be no hay in the field tomorrow.

I got out of the tractor and looked toward Highway 13, toward where I felt hot stares. A truck and two cars passed without the occupants looking my way. Still, I was the farmer who couldn't start a tractor and couldn't drive one either. Had I made the wrong decision by moving to the farm?

"Try it again," Jill said. "This time keep your wheels straight."

Fifteen minutes later, the tractor lunged to freedom. Not sure how. But it looked like I'd taken it mudding. It needed a trip to the carwash. My father would notice.

I shut the tractor off, feeling good about our accomplishments, considering the circumstances. The cows were huddled around the hay like coyotes around their kill. Ripping at the hay with their long tongues, munching down. Soon they would settle back into chewing their cuds.

We stood in the snow and watched, believing we might be farmers one day. But then we learned it was a business first and caretaking second. You can't save what you must sell. You can't sell what you must save. You can't serve God and mammon. This is the first hard lesson on the farm and in the world. You can't serve two masters.

But you must.

Serve two masters.

You must be present in the world and not be of it.

This is the hell of living in the world—living in the world's system.

It's hard to find pleasure in it.

Then I became the owner of my first calf.

What Lewis F. Allen said: *It may be asked, is beauty of form a highly desirable quality in an eat animal? Most certainly. But the eye and the judgment must be educated to know in what that beauty consists.*[4]

Once my father returned home from the hospital, Jill and I continued farming for them. We'd conquered the tractor and how to stab a roll of hay. I'd made progress while Jill kept opening gates and helping me pour pellets in the troughs. We enjoyed the way the cows bawled for hay and pellets. Rushing us along like impatient patrons at a diner. And we discovered "range cubes" around this time, which are pellets that have been produced in a large round cube that can be placed on the ground when troughs aren't feasible. But we used the range cubes to handfeed them through the fence. Some were hesitant to trust our hand in the beginning. They would shake their heads up and down as if to say, "Just place it on the ground. They go on the ground, you dummy." But we kept at it each day until most all eat out of our hands today. There are still a few holdouts that still like them on the ground. But we've turned the barnyard into a petting zoo, which infuriates my father because they run to the barn and bawl mercilessly each time they see anyone.

My stepmother told us to pick out a calf for helping them while my father was in the hospital. I was going to own a cow! And I felt great responsibility to choose the best one. I surveyed the herd for a week before I finally announced my selection, which would be like one of them hitting the cow lottery, because we would spoil the calf. We knew we would. And I chose a red one with a white forehead and a splotch of white beneath one eye that looked like a teardrop. She had been following me around the barnyard and butting me as if she wanted to play, as if I was one of them. But I made her one of us. This is what my father says, anyway. He says I've spoiled her, and I have. I feed her pellets off to the side and away from the herd. I named her "Teardrop," and made sure she knew her name. Today, you can shout her name and she will look up and find you, but not all is well with her.

Not everything has been easy with Teardrop. She is two years old now and still without calf. Everything I own becomes blemished it seems. My luck is horrible, if there is such a thing. I had Cowboy Tommy—a local legend in the cow business—check her and he felt around inside and said, "Her ovaries are small. She'll probably never calve."

Once my father heard this, he immediately wanted to sell Teardrop.

"I can't sell my first cow," I said.

She had become like a pet, which is not want you want to do with a beef cow.

My father said, "Well, we can't have a cow that can't calve."

"I'm not selling her," I said.

"Don't be silly," he said. "You can't keep a cow as a pet."

The Farm

I'd been worrying about Teardrop for a couple of months before Cowboy Tommy checked her. One day I researched how much it would cost to keep a cow as a pet. The only thing I could find in comparison was the cost of owning a dog or a cat. Over the lifetime of the dog, pet owners will pay approximately $25,000.[5] Seems outrageous, right? And considering the cow lives twice as long as a dog, a cow could cost upward of $20,000 over a 25-year period. Maybe more. My father had a point when he said her value was in the beef. I know keeping her is a huge financial commitment.

Cowboy Tommy said, "We can give her a hormone shot and see what happens. I've seen it work before."

My father said, "Okay, you get one year. If she hasn't had a calf in a year, she's going to be a steak dinner on a plate."

I took my chances.

Cowboy Tommy gave her the shot.

Now Teardrop is on the clock.

Other than my father needing my help, I moved to the farm because of job burnout. I worked at a psych hospital with suicidal adolescents who seemed to be on the clock. You never knew when they would end their lives, and we felt immense pressure to uproot the problem before insurance companies discharged them for no longer showing symptoms. But it's easy to show no symptoms in a psych hospital, but it's a different story back in the world where they came from. This is the ever-present danger with suicidal adolescents. They usually attempt more than once.

At the psych hospital, I ran a writing workshop for the suicidal adolescents. They arrived from their local ERs to the psych hospital. Their arms mutilated. Their minds tortured with self-hate. Some were gothic, others only misfits who were picked on at school. Some taken from their homes by DHR, betrayed by drug-addicted parents. It exposed deep emotional wounds—physical abuse, rape, a broken relationship, or parental hate. Their stay was short. Usually three or four days. But, still, they felt like lunatics, losers, the lost, the damned. And it was my job to build self-confidence as the insurance clock ticked. We never knew how many days the insurance companies would give us.

Mental health workers are constantly drained of their own sanity. I couldn't take sad stories anymore. Over a seven-year period, I'd taught 3,640 suicidal adolescents. I'd read 14,560 short stories and poems and published 225 issues of a literary magazine filled with these stories and poems. With at least three of my former students committing suicide after they left the hospital, I felt myself going down, as if I wasn't making a difference, so I retreated to the farm.

Before I was the writing teacher at the psych hospital, I was a psych tech, which meant I got the dirty work. If the psych patient puked, I cleaned it up. If they got confused and wandered into the wrong room, I retrieved them. I took them to the nameplate outside their door and said, "This is your room. See. This is your name." I took them out to smoke. I demonstrated the lighter on the wall of the smoking porch. No other lighters allowed. They could burn the place down. I followed the patients around the unit with a clipboard and a sheet with their name at the top. I marked their whereabouts every fifteen minutes, a record proving they were still alive. I announced snack time and led them to the snack room like a death march—heavy breathing, constant coughing, continuous moaning, bones creaking, gas slipping, feet shuffling, stomachs gurgling, and mouths drooling. It was all so heartbreaking, so after three years of it, I approached the senior therapist on the adolescent unit. I told him I would like to start a creative writing workshop for the suicidal adolescents at the hospital that combined writing and counseling, focusing on what they are saying about themselves through the characters in their stories. Hospital administration gave me three months to see if the adolescents would like such a class. It lasted seven years.

I taped pictures on a whiteboard in the classroom that I'd cut from *The New Yorker* magazine and from the *NY Times*—pictures that illustrated the fiction written and reviewed within their pages. On the backs of the pictures, I'd written a set of writing prompts.

They chose a picture, and I set a cooking timer to twenty minutes and said, "Go."

One teenage girl arrived at 4:30 in the morning with a three-inch bruise encircling her neck. A ring of fire. The perfect imprint of the belt. She hung herself after her boyfriend broke up with her. Fortunately, her mother found her swinging from her closet rod and called 911 while her stepfather cut the belt from around her neck. She was not breathing. Who knows how long she'd been unconscious?

The mother and stepfather gave her CPR. Her stepfather's lips upon her mouth.

Breathing for her.
Compression.
Breathing for her.
Compression.
Breathing for her.
Compression.
Her lungs filling.

A cough, then she began breathing on her own. Her enormous eyes opened. The shock setting in. She was still here. Earth remained her home when she no longer wanted to be a part of it.

She glanced out the large plate glass window in my classroom, out to the Beltline highway that cut through the center of the industrial city with its smokestacks and pollution on the river. Then she looked back at the other eight suicidal adolescents sitting around the table. It was as if she might be planning her escape, as if she was getting her bearings, getting a mental grid of the place. This fence leads to the road, that fence leads to the woods and that leads to freedom.

"I can't believe I'm here," she said when I asked her a question.

One of the other adolescents said, "It's not a bad place. You'll get used to it."

The teen that had answered the bruised-neck girl had been at the hospital for a week. Her mother was an alcoholic and couldn't care for her properly, so she lived with her grandmother. And she too wanted to die. She attempted what the rest of them had as well.

Now she was bubbly. She always wanted to help fold and bind the forthcoming book we published each week. We'd just finished Issue 43.

The bruised-neck girl attempted to clarify what she meant when she said, "I can't believe I'm here." She said, "No, not here in this hospital. I mean in this world."

We were quiet. We could only stare at her. I asked her to pull her hair back so I could see her neck better. She revealed where the belt had been. We craned forward to get a better look. It was a splotchy bruise. But defined. A belt had been there. No doubt.

She put her palms to her cheeks and said, "My face . . . It's so bruised."

"Does it hurt," I asked.

"No, it's swollen," she said.

Her cheeks were like puffy, grayish-blue clouds.

"I know you must be tired. I hear you had a long night. Are you sure you can write me a story?"

She didn't hesitate to answer. "I can write," she said.

She went to the board and chose the picture of a girl leaning against a farm utility truck—a picture I'd cut from the *New Yorker* magazine. She read the suggestions on the back. My suggestion was to write a story about a runaway girl. She wrote a half page, then turned her head and looked out the window, watching the cars snaking along the beltline. Then she said, "I must lie down."

I had a tech take her back to the unit.

Later that day, I looked out a door that opened upon the courtyard in the middle of the hospital. I noticed her standing in the window of her room with a fist of curtains in each hand, peering out, looking at nothing. Just existing there. In the window.

I sent a psych tech to check on her.

A week later, the bruise on her neck had diminished somewhat. She was better—smiling and writing stunning stories. On the day she was being discharged, she handed me a note.

I took it and read:

Mr. Robert:
Your class freakin' rocks! I have so much fun in there that all my problems disappear for those few hours. Thank you.

"That's so sweet of you," I said, closing the note.

"It's true," she said.

I watched her leave the hospital with her mother and stepfather, who probably combed the house for things that might double for a noose. They'll probably never look at a belt in the same way, and I knew they wouldn't sleep soundly for a few weeks. Maybe never again.

Her note gave me assurance that my class was working. I longed to create a place where they belonged, to create a space in my classroom free of judgment. A place of possibility in a non-threatening atmosphere where hope could begin. Enough room to move around in, so they could get back to their real selves. Whatever that may be. And I experienced this kind of assurance many times over the seven-year period. The class was a huge success, winning awards in the mental health world. Then I stopped believing in the system. It happened when a girl who peed in a bucket was admitted.

Emily lived with her aunt because her parents were addicts. But her aunt had reasons not to trust Emily. She was prone to run away, so her aunt did the drastic thing. She locked Emily in her bedroom after school with a padlock on the outside. Emily used a bucket for a latrine. She dumped it in the morning, then she showered, dressed, and went to school. This was the life she had decided to run from many times, but her latest run got her admitted to the psych hospital when Child Services got involved.

I asked, "How do you pass the time in your room?"

She said, "I read."

"What do you read?"

"Different stuff, but my aunt doesn't want me reading too much. So I have to sneak library books from school into my room. I slip them inside my binder because my aunt never checks it."

"That's smart," I said.

She smiled.

"Okay, show us the picture you chose, and then you can begin reading your story," I said.

It was a picture of a girl with a sad face sitting on her bed. I'd written on the back, "Why is this girl so sad? What happened?"

"It's sort of a true story, I guess," she said.

"Okay, go for it."

She said, "I see my father in every scar on my body. Deeper I go, looking, further into the vortex of tissue, every vein emitting little cries for him."

When she finished, I said, "I like what you're doing with the imagery. Where is your father? Is he still alive? Do you get to see him?"

"He lives in Michigan. Somewhere. My aunt gave me his phone number once, but he never answers my calls. He's messed up on drugs."

She scanned the faces at the table.

"So why are you here?"

"Cutting and running away," she said.

"Let me see your arms."

She pulled one sleeve of her hoodie up. She rolled her arm over, revealing hundreds of cuts—fresh and old.

"Who else cuts in here?"

All of them revealed their forearms. It was as if they'd survived a bus crash and every arm had traveled through shattered glass to be there. I looked around the table at them.

"I cut my legs, too," Emily said. "Want to see?" She raised her pant leg to reveal cuts on her calf, on her shin.

"Does that say *hate*?" I asked.

"Yeah, I was mad when I did that. It says *lie* over here, see?"

The following day, staff confiscated a screw from Emily. She'd worked for hours to unscrew it from a cabinet that was bolted to the wall in her room. Each room had two beds, two cabinets, two nightstands for their possessions, and one bathroom for every two rooms. The mirror was made from some type of reflective metal, a sink, a toilet, a shower—the bare necessities.

The screw that was confiscated from Emily took a special tool to loosen or tighten it. Only the maintenance man could work these screws, so we thought. And no matter how hard staff tried to safeguard these rooms, the adolescents always found something to cut themselves with.

She hid in her room, using the screw like a nine-inch nail. Then she passed the screw around to the other adolescents, like a joint, like a fifth of wine. Making blood pacts.

Staff gave the place a good old prison shakedown. Every article of clothing was searched. Every bed overturned. Dust mites danced in the light streaming from the windows. But there was only the lone screw of communion, and once we confiscated it, the community died.

The psychiatrist placed Emily in the observation room and took her clothes away. They dressed her in a yellow, paper gown. A staff person sat in the doorway 24/7, to make sure she no longer cut herself. But mostly it was for punishment.

I went to the observation room to check on her each day, wondering what I could say to convince her that her father was in Michigan, not deep within a cut on her body.

Emily's isolation lasted 24 hours. Now she sat at my table in the classroom. The twenty-minute writing exercise was over, and Emily wanted to read first. She held up the picture she had chosen of a black forest. Her story was about a train in a black forest that searched for runaway girls in the night.

When she finished, I said, "Wow! That was great."

The other adolescents around the table agreed.

I said, "What's the inspiration behind it?"

"Before my aunt started locking me in my room, I ran away and walked to the train track behind our house in the woods. Determined to throw myself in front of a train. But I couldn't do it. I just sat there all night in the woods at the edge of our neighborhood, watching each train pass, carrying with it my opportunity to die. I couldn't do it. The police found me walking through our neighborhood."

The insurance company finally discharged Emily after 21 days, which was one of the longer stays at the hospital. Child Services needed time, but they hadn't discovered enough evidence to remove her from the aunt's home, and the psychiatrist didn't want Emily to know she was leaving until the moment her aunt walked into the lobby to retrieve her. He was afraid she would react badly to the news, so Emily didn't know what I knew when she finished reading the story of the black forest. It would be her last one in my class. The aunt would come for her that afternoon with the key to the padlock in her pocket. And I wanted to tell Emily, "You're leaving today, and I wish it were not so. But you take care. I will miss you. Keep writing. I think you have a future as a writer." But I had to play the psychiatrist's dirty game. I got paid to follow a plan I didn't always agree with.

I wasn't around when Emily was discharged.

Later, I asked the nurse what had happened.

I asked, "Did she leave without fighting them?"

"She was crying," the nurse said. "But she went without a fight."

I imagined the ride home with the aunt. The yelling, the accusations, then the closing of her bedroom door, the snap of the padlock, the bucket on the floor, the bitterness, the lone train whistle in the black forest behind her house.

What the Misfit in Flannery O'Conner's story said: *It's no real pleasure in life.*[6]

Somehow, at such a young age, they believed the Misfit's lie. And by the end, I was overcome by their sadness. I stopped believing I could make a difference. For even psych hospitals can become toxic places, and the Misfit's lie finally pushed me out the door and to the farm.

Coconut

1978

I met an orphan boy who lived at the Baptist Children's Home in Brentwood, Tennessee halfway through our freshman year at Franklin High School. Both his parents had died of cancer, leaving him no options. Everyone called him "Coconut" because his little round head—sporting an afro—looked just like a coconut. We hit it off the first time we met and started hanging out together. He talked sense to my mixed-up mind. He had it together and didn't play the victim. Life couldn't seemingly knock him down. I respected this and needed this kind of grit.

Coconut didn't have a driver's license. He never needed one. He knew he could count on me to take him places in my 1967 Firebird. Plus, he always listened when I talked. I'd never had that. We shared everything and spent our time cruising around a small town that was once the bloodiest terrain in the Civil War. Thirty percent of the advancing Confederate army decimated. One of only a few Civil War battles that continued after dark. But we cared nothing for this bloody campaign. We cared nothing for the broken statue on the square. Erected in 1899 by the United Daughters of the Confederacy. Made from Italian marble, with a granite base. They stitched together quilts in lamp light and sold them to purchase the statue they nicknamed "Chip," because the brim of his hat had been broken off by a guide rope when they erected him. I had circled him thousands and thousands of times, never knowing this about him. I never even looked up, only out the windshield of my 1967 Firebird. But the whole town has a history of brokenness. And we were trapped in the loop. We cruised where men once feared to march. We weren't searching for a cause. We just wanted to belong to something, even if that something was unified motion, a gravitational pull around a city built for such circular activity.

Of all the things that drove us hoodlums to the streets of Franklin, the most common was a lack of a home life. We roamed the town like it was our house. Into the living room of the town square, down the hallway of Main Street, and through the bedroom subdivisions and shopping centers, stopping every now and then in the kitchen of a gas station and a restaurant. But mainly we kept moving, because to stop brought the silence we feared.

Coconut and I never left home without a clean Firebird—inside and out. This was my goal in life. Keep a clean car and attract attention. I wanted everyone to know I had a badass car. Its previous owner had turned it into a dragster. It still had a line lock installed, which is a device that allows the front brakes to lock independently of the rear brakes via a switch, allowing a burnout with the rear wheels. It was fast. Stupid fast. And loud with cherry bomb mufflers. Painted a beautiful blue. Everything about the Firebird was exquisite. Performance and looks to boot. It was a head-turner. The perks of my father owning an auto parts store. That car was my reputation. It was my real home. The only place I could call a real home, anyway. And it belonged to me, and Coconut and I lived in it.

What Walter Russell Bowie said: *The feeble life is that which has no stronghold at all, and has never bravely undertaken the task of building one. It submits with passivity to the chances of its existence.*[7]

Coconut was a drummer but didn't have a drum set. He couldn't afford one. But he carried drumsticks in his back pocket. And wherever we partied, we'd line whiskey bottles, beer cans, plastic milk jugs, tin coffee cans, anything that would make a noise when banged, then we'd turn him loose. Man, could he bang. And we'd sit and listen with rap attention and pass joint after joint. Then we'd put on AC/DC or Van Halen, and he'd play along. Making every lick.

When AC/DC's 1979 *Highway to Hell* tour came to Nashville's Municipal Auditorium, we bought tickets. Angus Young mesmerized us as he stomped across the stage, making his signature guitar licks. We had never seen anything like him. The next day at Franklin High— standing behind the yellow stripe the school maintenance man had painted behind the school to designate the smoking area—we smoked a quick cigarette before class. Still about half intoxicated. And all the little hoodlums like us had on their AC/DC T-shirts with Angus Young and those devil's horns on the front and "I'm on the Highway to Hell" on the back. We had felt something the night before, but we did not know it would feel like camaraderie the next day, and I never felt it again at school.

What M. Scott Peck said: *The great enemy of community is exclusivity.*[8]

By my freshman year of high school, the supervisor and my mother moved out of their apartment and purchased a house in an upscale subdivision outside of Franklin. My mother said she had a room for me. That I could move in with them and have my own bedroom. But I knew the supervisor didn't want me there, so for the first month I floated back and forth between my father's house and theirs. Then I told my mother I would stay if she'd let Coconut move in with us. I couldn't let him live at the Baptist Children's Home. Seemingly alone—there inside religious trappings. I couldn't bear the thought of it. Then again, my situation might not have been any better, because of the supervisor. But my mother was desperate to prove to family and others that she hadn't abandoned her son, that she could win back his affection, so she agreed, even though the supervisor was against it. He said to me, "Is this your little trick, huh? You think I can't see what you're doing here."

"What?" I said. "You don't feel sorry for him?"

I'm still not clear on what he thought I was doing. Maybe trying to spoil his tryst with my mother. And from that day forward, the supervisor longed for a reason to kick both of us out.

What George Armatage said: *Cows have a curious fashion, sometimes, of hiding out their calves. When a cow with a young calf starts for water she invariably hides her calf in a bunch of grass or clump of bushes in some secluded spot, where it lies down and remains perfectly quiet until the mother returns. The calf under such circumstances seems to understand that it is "not at home," and cannot be seen.*

One night, Coconut and I purchased some blotter acid and floated out past the idiotic Confederacy, beyond the Civil War statue on the square, across seven seas, underneath the strong arm of reason, out past the gulf, where we laughed and laughed. A thousand heads poking out of foxholes, their round mouths forming, their eyes like marbles, their voices pounding like heavy artillery. Then snorting horses with the smell of bloody rawhide chased us back from the wasteland, and we desperately sought a party. We needed to be around real people.

Coconut hung his head outside the Firebird every now and then and yelled at people sitting around the square. "Hey, where's the party?"

Finally, someone told us about one spread across a bush-hogged field on the outskirts of Franklin. Approaching, we saw a bonfire burning. I parked a good distance away from the bonfire. I didn't want any ash settling on the Firebird.

We walked upon the inner circle of people who sat drinking and passing a joint. To the right of us, sat two kegs hooked up to tavern nozzles, floating in a tub of ice. Draft beer always seemed to taste bitter to me. I guess I preferred the Miller ponies. They came in a neat little eight-pack with a handle on top and fit the palm of your hand so that you could bang a stop sign as you whizzed by.

New people arrived, as old ones left leaving a dust trial. Coconut and I were making our rounds. He popped a Quaalude into his mouth and bent under the tap of the keg and held an open mouth beneath the flow of beer. It ran down the sides of his face and into his nappy hair that soaked it up like a sponge.

I knew it was time to leave the party when Coconut fell more than he stood, so I told him, "Let's go."

He said, "Yes, let's go. I'm freezing out here."

We walked through the field toward the Firebird, stumping our toes and stumbling every now and then in a rut. Then I saw the Firebird and said, "There she is."

We climbed inside and fired the engine. I turned the heater full blast. Coconut's teeth were chattering.

"I've never been this cold," he said.

The Marshall Tucker Band was lightly playing on WKDF out of Nashville, and we rumbled back across the cattleguard at the edge of the field. Coconut held up his cup of beer to keep from spilling it.

"This stuff tastes like crap," he said.

"Strange for you to say. You couldn't keep your mouth off the spigot."

He laughed and let out a whoop. I smiled and shook my head.

He rolled down his window and chucked the beer—cup and all—out the window.

"I can't believe you just did that," I said. "Now I have beer all down the side of my car."

"Sorry. I wasn't thinking."

The low-lying fog rushed past the headlights as Coconut struggled to find the music he wanted. He kept pulling cassettes out and shoving them back inside the case. He finally settled on Van Halen. His favorite.

We rumbled into the supervisor's driveway with Coconut singing Van Halen. He made reckless drum licks on my dashboard. After I shut the car off, he kept singing and banging. I told him, "We're home."

He announced in a drunken whisper that he had to piss. I led him around to the side of the house, where he fought hard to stand, as he unzipped his pants. He secured his balance and gazed up at the stars.

He shouted, "Man, what relief!"

I said, "Shut-up! You're being loud."

Startled, he rocked back and forth on the balls of his heels. "Listen, don't tell me to shut-up."

I heard the front door of the house open. Pepper, the supervisor's miniature schnauzer, ran out and began to bark. We walked into the pallid porch light and startled the supervisor.

"What are you boys doing?"

Neither one of us responded. I knew he could smell the beer Coconut had bathed himself in.

"What have you boys been doing?"

"Nothing, just hanging out," I said.

He stared hard at Coconut.

I said, "We're going to bed."

"He's not staying here tonight," the supervisor said.

"Where's he supposed to stay? He lives here."

"Tonight, he doesn't."

"Why not?"

"He's drunk. And I don't want him in my house."

"Well, sorry. He lives here. Drunk or sober. It doesn't matter."

I tried to step inside.

The supervisor blocked the door. He said, "Drunk people don't live in my house."

"Well, this isn't YOUR house. We live here, too."

"I pay the bills around here, and you two hooligans aren't living here anymore. Go live with your father. See if he'll take the two of you in."

I thought, *Don't mess with us. Not tonight. Not anytime. Not ever.*

I clenched my fist and said, "You're not going to stop us from living here."

"What do you have in mind?" the supervisor said.

I turned to Coconut. "Let's go to bed."

I tried to step inside again, but the supervisor caught me by the shoulder and spun me around. This was when I dry-gulched him. I hit him in the side of the head. He stumbled backwards, shocked for a moment. Then he threw me out of the doorway and onto the driveway. I charged him and threw another punch. He punched back. We stood toe-to-toe throwing punches like two Olympian boxers. He swung. I swung. He connected. I connected. Then my mother came running out of the house and jumped on the supervisor's back.

"Stop! Stop!" she screamed.

The supervisor and I never let up, while my mother rode his back like a game of war-horse, slapping him in the head, trying to grab his arms, trying to hold him off.

What Emil Cioran said: *Only one thing matters: learning to be the loser.*[9]

I broke and ran to the Firebird. Coconut was too stunned to do anything but follow.

"Get in!" I yelled at Coconut.

He stumbled, then stumbled again. His feet would not obey. He kept looking back, looking back. Stumbling in a drunken stupor.

"Get in. Hurry. Just get in!" I shouted.

As we ran for the Firebird, the supervisor stopped his pursuit. Maybe he remembered he was a man and not a schoolboy. I don't know. But he stopped and stood panting in the driveway with his hands on his knees.

I cranked the motor. The Firebird rumbled. Cherry Bomb mufflers. Van Halen screaming again. Coconut beside me. The door open, his body halfway in and halfway out. I should've left, but I stopped in the driveway and ruthlessly cussed the supervisor. And it was too much for the man from Pennsylvania. He lunged toward the Firebird.

Before I could get it in gear, he reached through the window and grabbed a handful of my long hair. He pulled me out of the window. My body teetered between the car and the ground below. He delivered his best punches of the night. Then my mother jumped him from behind again. She held him long enough for me to drop back into the seat. I slammed it into first gear and let out the clutch. The tires spun and threw loose rocks against the side of the house.

When we reached the edge of the neighborhood, Coconut said, "Stop." He opened the door and puked.

Coconut and I decided to sleep in the car that night in front of my father's house, so we headed in that direction. He lived at the edge of a dead-end street. We could sit there undetected. We were exhausted and no longer tripping. It was late. The rooster had crowed three times. Everyone had either crashed or taken their partying to the fields. I steered the Firebird across the battlefield. Beneath low-hanging trees, casting shadows across our path. The red lights blinked. Red on one side. Yellow on the other. The town was a cautionary tale, like a fable had ended. The pumpkin smashed. Cinderella tucked in bed. The fairy godmother snoring in the pages of some library.

We parked in front of my father's house and sat there staring into the sky through the Firebird's windshield. Flakes of light flickered in the dark vault. We smoked the day's last cigarette. Lost. The glow of the streetlight at the end of the neighborhood spilled into the car.

Coconut said, "The day after we buried my father, my grandparents told us they couldn't take care of us. Then my brother and I were taken to the Baptist's Children's Home. I hated the place. I couldn't figure out why my mother was taken, then my father. What had I done to God to deserve it?"

I didn't say anything. I lit a joint and handed it to him.

He took it.

I shoved Bob Seger's *Live Bullet* into the tape deck. "Turn the Page" moaned, sweet, and low through the speakers. Coconut passed the joint to me and closed his eyes. His breathing seemed to be in rhythm with the song, as Seger sang about a lonesome highway and a page turning. Then the sun dawned, and the glow of the streetlight gave way to a light much brighter. And flickered off.

After the fight with the supervisor, my father sought renewed revenge. He hid in alleyways, behind parked cars at grocery stores, behind trees on side roads and outside the city limits. Watching for them, watching for the Corvette. Ready to repay him for hitting his son and for taking his wife. One night he caught the supervisor and my mother in front of the post office at Five Points, just off Main Street in Franklin. Not too far from J.B. Cook Auto Parts. He slugged the supervisor's driver's side window and the supervisor had him arrested.

What David Shields said: *As a work gets more autobiographical, more intimate, more confessional, more embarrassing, it breaks into fragments. Our lives aren't prepackaged along narrative lines and, therefore, by its very nature, reality-based art—underprocessed, underproduced—splinters and explodes.*[10]

After the night I fought the supervisor, he never spoke of the incident. Neither did my mother. Both afraid of my father. And soon the supervisor relented. He let us back in the house. It took us two days to gain reentry. And life went back to life. From that night forward, the supervisor and I barely spoke to one another. It took my mother twenty years for her to admit the fight even happened.

What George Armatage said: *It may here be remarked that on first leaving the cow-house, the calf should be confined in a safe place in the yard or elsewhere for a day or two, until it becomes accustomed to the bright light of day, as on its first introduction it appears almost blind, and would likely to run into danger.*[11]

I was fifteen when I hit a boy in the head with a motorcycle helmet in front of the Franklin Theatre on Main Street. The boy was beating up a friend of mine over some girl who had cheated on my friend. I was lucky it didn't kill him. He went down on one knee, and we jumped on my Honda motorcycle and fled down Main Street. Our reflection shapeshifting in the windows of the shops as we raced toward the square. My friend's arms around me, holding on for dear life. I could feel his body shaking. I even thought he was my brother, but soon I tried to pick a fight with him when he got back together with the girl who had cheated on him. An unresolved anger ran through the town and encouraged my own.

And you, you thought I was worthy of your compassion.

What the Gospel Singer once said: *Did you think I could be what you said I was? Didn't you know from your own black hearts what mine must be like?*[12]

Making Hay

2017

What George Armatage said: *Supposing a cow to be fed at the rate of 56 lbs. per day during 120 days, she will consume exactly three tons of hay.*[13]

My father and I make hay while the sun shines, if the baler doesn't breakdown. And on that June day—with 90° weather—the baler was broken down again. We stood beside it with greasy hands inside its innards. My father keeps a supply of bolts in a brown paper bag he uses to repair broken gears. That day, we broke bolts for every ten bales of hay. It's an ancient baler. Worn-out and insufferable. Too old for the 225 large rolls of hay we need each year for the 50-head of cattle. But it's all we can afford. A new one costs about $23,000. Small farms have a narrow margin of profit. One bad occurrence and we barely break even. So, buying a new baler is out of the question. And this is what makes my father so indispensable. He's an ace mechanic. He knows how to patch things and keep worn-out machinery running when most farmers would have to pay outrageous repair bills. He has the expertise that I don't possess. I do good to tighten a screw. On my own, I'm not a farmer.

Once we repaired the gear, we went to work on a wad of hay wrapped around a lower bar that pulls the hay from the field into the baler. That's all I can tell you about it. It's an important mechanism. But hay had it locked up. I'd never seen it this bad.

My father handed me a butcher knife and said, "Climb under there and cut it off."

I got on my knees, reached inside the baler and sawed across the hay that was thick like rope around the bar. It took us three hours to free the baler. We used a machete, a chainsaw, a lighter, and a putty knife. We were on our backs, our knees, our haunches. My father said we'd burn it if he had insurance.

It takes a man like my father to scratch and gouge a living out of farming. It takes worn-out equipment and the skill to patch it. I know each hay season could be the last with him. I think of this often. I try to enjoy the moment. Stay present and not complain. For, like the grass, it's all withering away. If my father dies, the cows will be sold. It would be like the whole family dying at once. We have grown to love the cows in this way. We've named them. We've nurtured their babies along with them. We've watched a few die on the farm. We even have a cemetery where we bury each one.

My father said, wiping his greasy hands on a rag, "Let's see how far we get this time." He climbed back inside the New Holland tractor that once had A/C in the cab. Now the A/C is broken, and we've removed both doors from the cab. I told him we should break out the front glass of the cab. He said flatly, "We can't do that."

He revved the engine. The gears in the baler clanked into motion and the large conveyor-like belts turned. He pulled away as dust puffed from the threadbare tires of the baler. I watched it vacuum up the hay. A new roll was taking shape, growing like a ball of yarn. Just how, I don't know. This is my problem.

A long bridge on Highway 13 covers a part of the field like a canopy. Birds nest underneath as log trucks rush downhill and across the surface, using their loud Jake brake that echoes in the hills and flutters across the field like a covey of quails. I looked toward the river where visitors at the Buffalo River Resort splashed in the water. The sound of joyful screams and splashing water converged above the river, while the clunking of oars against the hulls

Making Hay

of canoes knocked from the underworld. Across the river from our labor in the field, the world told a different narrative.

Each time the baler broke down, my father shouted at the field, "I'm gonna sell every cow and have a campground next year." And it would work. The resort is evidence across the way. But who in their right mind would trade cows for a bunch of drunken campers? Bawls are better than complaints and even better than the exuberance of those who litter the land, then go home to Nashville. Give me cows any day.

If there's one thing I like doing on the farm, then it's cutting hay and bush-hogging. Making straight lines in a field appeals to me. It's one thing I can control on the farm. But even this has taken time to learn. At first, I kept looking back over my shoulder to see if I was making a straight line, and every time I turned and looked back, I inadvertently tugged the wheel to the side, knocking the tractor off course. My father told me to never look back, but I reckon a person always has a notion to look over his shoulder.

It took a while, but I learned to bush-hog and cut hay without looking back. I learned to sight across the field at a distant point, be it a tree, a barn, a distant hill, or some other point, and keep the nose of the tractor squarely on the sighting point. Once I learned this, my lines were straighter than an arrow. My father even told me, "Son, you hold a pretty wheel. Even Dale Earnhardt wiggles the wheel every now and then. But you, you hold a pretty one."

But there's one thing I will do once my father is gone. I'll burn the baler. I'll sprinkle its ashes on a cowpat. I'll invest some money in a new one. Somehow.

What Joseph A. Munk said: *The average ranch is not intended to furnish luxuries, but to serve the best interests of the business in hand, that of growing cattle.*[14]

One day my father asked if I'd like to go to the stockyard and watch our calves being sold. I gave him a horrified look and said, "Why would I ever want to do that?"

Sometimes I imagine it. I see the scared calves being chased onto the stage of an auction. Running and stumbling around the interior of the stockyard as the auctioneer raps out some numbers, while farmers in overalls raise their hands. They buy them and finish them out. It's heart-breaking to think this is where we send them.

We make sure the herd is treated humanely. We let them roam like a herd. For this reason, our cows are on the wild side. My stepmother told us the cows have changed since Jill and I started working with them. She said they're not as aloof and jumpy. We make sure to walk among them each day. Sometimes I sing to them. Their ears twitch and raise. They seem to like interaction with humans. At first, they kept their heads and ears up. The calves all ran from us. Now they rarely raise their heads from grazing or get up from the places where they chew their cuds.

I read a study once about how dogs have developed a muscle that controls their inner eyebrow, allowing them to enlarge their eyes, making them appear like an infant's—those puppy-dog eyes. They believe it developed out of a need to communicate with humans. And I get the same feeling while looking at cows. Their eyes draw me in like puppy-dog eyes. Those long eyelashes and the way they look droopy-eyed and serene while chewing their cuds. This interaction makes it hard when we betray their trust by selling their babies.

The first time we helped my father sell his calves, we poured beef pellets in the troughs inside the corrals. Once the pellets were consumed, we led the mothers out and corralled the calves. Then Cowboy Tommy, who hauls our cattle to the Dickson Cattle Auction, backed his truck up to the barn. We ran them onto his trailer. I could hear them bawling when he pulled onto Highway 13. I should have known better than naming one of the bull calves "Kaliga." He was gentle. He ate range cubes out of my hand and followed me around the barnyard. Had I trained him to be led to the slaughter? Had I quit my job and sold my house for this? Jill and I knew farms brought life, but we didn't realize they caused death. Farms have an underworld.

MAKING HAY

That night, clouds rushed over the farm, scraping across a full moon, like leaves dragging over a boulder in a running creek. Rushing forward. Everything continuing. Life is continuation in the face of death. The farm teaches you this. The unborn calf awaits his fate. And you will assist him in it. This is the hell I found in farming. Cows are born, they die, then they come back as steak dinners and hamburgers. But the farm must continue. My father and stepmother have bills to pay. The cows pay the bills. They keep the farm running. But business doesn't keep the mothers from roaming the farm looking for their calves, bawling over the fences as if their calves will come running. They always believe their babies are still on the farm. Out there somewhere. Just out of earshot range. But the stockyard is 30 miles away. This is what's so heartbreaking.

I watched them a while, wondering what you do to console a cow. I did not Google-it, instead I did what we usually do for those who grieve. I put out three bales of hay and told them, "Y'all come eat. You need to eat." They continued to bawl and roam. They stood in different corners of the pasture and bawled over the fences. I apologized profusely, as if they knew I had something to do with the disappearance of their babies.

That night, after Cowboy Tommy had dropped off the calves in Dickson, the bawling on the farm continued as the moon passed over the fields like a searchlight.

What Mahatma Gandhi said: *Ahimsa is the highest duty. Even if we cannot practice it in full, we must try to understand its spirit and refrain as far as is humanly possible from violence.*[15]

I wondered what the cows said about us, if they said anything at all. "You got to watch the farmer. They'll mess you up every time. Ain't met a farmer yet that won't steal your babies."

Yet, I never sensed the cows held it against me.

Brentwood Girls

1978

Our junior year of high school started two months after the fight with the supervisor. And at the beginning of each year, the cheerleaders were chosen by the school body. We'd assemble inside the gym and wait for the wanna-be-cheerleaders to come running from a side door into the gym. One at a time. Tumbling and screaming, "Go Rebels." With numbers pinned to their shirts to identify them.

I wasn't as into it as Coconut. I knew I didn't stand a chance with any of them. But it was time away from class. For Coconut, it was a time to catch a glimpse of the incoming freshmen girls that were trying out for the squad.

We made our way to the top of the bleachers, as Coconut talked about it being the best crop of freshmen girls. "Franklin girls don't have anything to match the Brentwood girls," he said.

Brentwood, Tennessee was barely on the map back then and didn't have a high school, so all the Brentwood kids drove to Franklin High in their BMWs and new convertible sportscars. They looked like fashion models in their designer clothes and eyewear.

Things are much different now. Nashville gets 100 new people a day moving into the greater-Nashville area and the suburbs beyond. High schools dot the landscape like coffee shops. But in the

1970s, we all attended one high school. The rich and the poor, the hoodlums and the dorks, the Brentwoodians and the Franklinites. One big mix.

I sat beside him doodling the names of rock bands on my jeans with an ink pen. The latest was *Van Halen*. I'd finished *Journey* that morning in class.

"Get a look at her," Coconut said when the first Brentwood girl ran across the gym—tumbling and screaming and waving her pom-poms. "That's who I'm voting for," Coconut said.

"You don't stand a chance," I said.

"Brentwood girls love the 'fro," he said, patting the sides of his afro.

"That they do," I said.

He whistled when she finished. He had the most shrilling whistle, the kind that stripped paint from walls.

I looked up from doodling on my jeans as the next girl performed her routine. There was something about her. You could tell she was nervous, that she had put a lot into rehearsing her routine, almost to the point of making it seem robotic. But there were moments of grace, too. Moments when she let her guard down and shot the sweetest smile. A Mariah Carey smile. Innocent and fresh.

"Who is that?" I asked Coconut.

"Jill Whitehurst," he said. "Her older sister is Gwen."

I knew Gwen. She was the captain of the cheerleading squad my freshman year.

Coconut turned toward me and squared his shoulders. He looked me in the eyes. "I see who you'll be voting for."

I smiled.

He said, "See. I told you you'd like this."

But I knew I'd never appear on Jill's radar. I was the boy in remedial classes with rock bands doodled on his jeans and concert T-shirts for a wardrobe. I was the addlebrained boy on drugs who fell asleep on my desk from the valium I'd stolen from my mother—her drug of choice back then. I hung-out behind the school smoking cigarettes between classes. Talking cheap. We knew we were white trash from the trailer park or small ranch houses.

45

I kept my eyes on Jill as she finished her tryout.
The way she jumped.
The way she jabbed the world.
The slight jerks.
The rhythm of her hair.
The way it flew away, and then came gracefully down across her face.
One hand on her hip.
Hips squared.
Arm above her.
Pom-pom raised.
That smile at the end of the cheer.
I never took my eyes from her.

Then I attended every ballgame after she made the squad. I even drove past her house a few times. Coconut knew where she lived. The Baptist Children's Home was in Brentwood, and he had attended Brentwood Junior High.

That year, when Jill made the homecoming court, I cutout a picture of her from Franklin, Tennessee's local newspaper, *The Review Appeal*. Her sister was the homecoming queen and Jill was on the court. In the picture, Jill stood with her father on the football field wearing a crown—smiling. She always smiled at everyone. Seemed approachable. But I was shy. Stupefied shy. Afraid of what Jill might think of my family and our neighborhood, about me as a person. Plus, I didn't trust girls and never made one move toward getting to know Jill.

Still, I pinned the picture to the wall in my bedroom at the supervisor's house. Near my Farrah Fawcett swimsuit poster. Both were out of reach, but Farrah talked back to me. She gave me motherly advice. And now I had a mother-figure and a girlfriend on the wall and not once thought of it as crazy, only safe.

What Cormac McCarthy said: *But someplace in the scheme of things this world must touch the other.*[16]

Wide Awake

1979

One day I heard moans coming from downstairs at the supervisor's house. My mother's moans. I stood at the top of the stairs, undetected. My mother was on her knees begging the supervisor not to leave her. He relented for a few more months.

What Dietrich Bonhoeffer said: *Indeed the tempter is only to be found where there is innocence; for where there is guilt, he has already gained power.*[17]

The Phone Number

1979

October turned to November. Football season was almost over. Coconut and I stood against the wall at the top of the football stadium. Up where we could smoke and watch the girls. Mostly I watched Jill. Far enough away that she couldn't see my eyes. She never looked to where the hoodlums gathered.

At halftime, everyone went to the restrooms behind the bleachers or stood outside to talk in the shadows. A bunch of cheerleaders were standing in line at the concession stand on the far end. I was trying to see if Jill was one of them when I walked right into her by mistake as she was coming out of the restroom. I grabbed her and took a couple of short steps with her in my arms, trying to keep her from falling. Then we both looked at one another. I was no more than a foot away from her. She smiled and pulled at the hem of her cheerleading skirt that rustled in the blustery Tennessee night, and I held her there, not wanting to let go.

"Sorry," she said with a smile on her face.

Then she stepped away from me and walked toward the concession stand, where she turned and looked back at me once she joined the line.

What Richard Rohr said: *From inside experience, you know God's love is a tender dance of give-and-take, rescue and holding.*[18]

The Phone Number

I cruised by Jill's house after the football game that night, smoking weed. Coconut had left the game with other friends. I felt lonely. My Firebird rumbling down her street. The moon in the trees, casting shadows over my journey. I drove to her, and then away. Shadows sweeping past.

I knew I had to figure out a way to contact her. Coconut told one of her friends that I wanted to go out with Jill. The friend laughed and said I didn't stand a chance, but she would ask.

The next day she handed Coconut Jill's home phone number. Coconut handed it to me and said, "She said call her."

"Call who?" I took the number and saw Jill's name above the number.

Coconut slapped me on the back and let out one of his whoops.

A smile cracked my face.

But I could never get the courage to dial the last digit. I'd get to this point, then hang up. I called a few times while Coconut watched and shook his head in disbelief. "Just call her," he said, "or I will."

"May I speak to Jill?" I said, when she answered. I could feel my face flush. I could barely breathe.

"This is she," she said.

"This is Robbie," I said.

"I hoped you'd call," she said.

Her voice seemed softer. Almost as if she were shy. But it was probably because she wasn't yelling a cheer. That was the only other time I'd really heard her voice.

"So, what are you doing?" I said.

"Well, right now I'm watching television."

"That's cool."

It went on like this for a while. Just small talk, then she asked, "What kind of music do you like?"

I panicked. I didn't want her to know that I listened to mostly southern rock, such as Marshall Tucker, Lynyrd Skynyrd, and The

Allman Brothers Band. I thought she might even dislike rock and think I was weird. So I said, "I like disco."

She laughed. "You like to dance? I would have never thought that."

"Yeah, me either. I guess dancing just takes you away." *Takes you away!* I couldn't believe what came out of my mouth. I spoke quickly, trying to erase the comment. "What about you?"

"No, I don't care much about disco. I usually listen to Kansas, Boston, stuff like that."

"Yeah, me too. I mean, I like all kinds of music. I go to concerts all the time."

"Who've you seen lately?"

"Uh . . . let's see. The last concert I went to was AC/DC."

"Wow! Now that's different from disco. You do like all kinds if you like disco and AC/DC."

We lapsed into silence. It was time for the question. I couldn't hold it inside any longer. "Well, I was a wondering if you'd like to go out Friday night?"

"Sure, but I have a football game. Can we go somewhere after the game?"

"Yeah, that would be great."

"Just come to the game, and we'll talk about it from there."

"Sounds good," I said.

"I'll be looking for you," she said.

I hung up and shouted, "Yes!"

Brown Sugar

2017

What Lewis F. Allen once said: *The stomach of a calf being very delicate, it is most easily affected by any change, and scouring soon follows a little fasting aggravated by the irritation and fear of losing its mother, which often retards the growth of young calves for several weeks, if it does not cost their lives.*[19]

Brown Sugar is a scrappy calf. Her mother belonged to my grandfather who died in the year 2000. Now Brown Sugar's mother is twenty-three. The oldest cow on the farm. She's my granddaughter's favorite. She named her Big Mama, and my granddaughter was excited when she heard Big Mama had delivered a baby. She named her Brown Sugar because she is a dirty blonde color. We let my granddaughter name a few of the new calves, which all have something to do with food—for some reason. There's Cookie, Marshmallow, Fudge Brownie, and other calves that have been sold. We tell her the calves are sold to other farms. How can you tell a child that Marshmallow was shot in the head? So, for our own mental health, and for hers, we tell sweet little lies.

We have a few deadbeat cows. They look at the bull as if to say, "Enough already. Give an old cow a break. Just one year. That's all I ask. Just one year to exist without having the life sucked out of me." I'm sure some long for retirement and long to have their teats back. We had one a few weeks back give birth, and then decide she was going to lie down and have a smoke break and a cup of coffee before she licked her calf dry. The calf shivered in the cold wind. We dried it for her.

But Brown Sugar's mother has been a good mother, even though she's advancing in years. Unable to produce enough milk for Brown Sugar, we started supplementing with a bottle. Every morning and evening, we went to the pasture and called her name. "Come get your bottle Brown Sugar." And she would run to us and down the bottle in thirty seconds flat. We loved those moments with her and miss them now that she's a young heifer. I can only image how hard that must have been for Brown Sugar to accept the bottle. She had to go against her nature. And if Brown Sugar had tried reasoning herself to that bottle, then she would have told herself the bottle was not her mother's teat, and, therefore, could not nourish her. But somewhere along the way she realized she would not survive the natural way. She needed outside assistance. She would have starved without it, so we nurtured her with the bottle.

For this reason, I was shocked the day my father wanted to sell Brown Sugar. It's the misfits I love. Plus, we had invested so much in her. But she had had a stillborn calf. Maybe she was too young to be a mother when it happened. This sort of thing happens when you allow the herd to be the herd and never separate the bull. Young heifers get pregnant before their time. And I spotted Brown Sugar at the top of the highest point of the farm on a hillside, away from the herd, which is usually a sign they've given birth. They hide their babies for two days from everyone. They even eat their own afterbirth to keep predators away. Then they rejoin the herd after a few days. So, I went to where she grazed and looked for the calf. I found it still wrapped in the placenta. "Oh, Brown Sugar," I said mournfully. I felt if I had been there sooner there might have been something I could've done. I felt negligent. But the calf was tiny. Maybe premature. I couldn't tell and couldn't ask my father who was out of town. He'd left me in charge of the farm for a month, and this happened the last day. Everything was going great. I'd fared well until that moment.

I buried the calf in the cemetery.

My father returned from his trip.

Life continued.

Now he wanted to sell Brown Sugar, which he had never mentioned to me. I thought we were selling the calves only. I knew a few had to go. We had too many. The whole farm had been grazed down to a nub. My father was waiting for beef prices to go up. They kept declining and my father kept stalling, hoping the market would rebound. But prices remained low.

Cowboy Tommy always comes on Mondays. The sale is every Tuesday. In winter, we gather the calves on Sunday and put them in the barn overnight. But in the summer heat we wait until the last moment on Monday. And the Monday my father tried to sell Brown Sugar a torrential downpour moved into the area that morning. I was sure my father would wait and sell the following week, but he called at 6 a.m. and wanted my help. I tried to talk him out of selling for a week, but he reminded me that the stockyard would be closed the following week due to the 4th of July holiday and that would mean we would have to wait two more weeks. So, I reluctantly went to the barn to help.

My father stood at the gate to the pen shaking a pot of beef pellets, trying to lure the ones he wanted inside the pen. Brown Sugar had fallen for the trap. I walked to where he stood and asked if he planned to sell Brown Sugar.

"She had a stillborn. She's got to go."

"You can't sell Brown Sugar. That's Pap's calf," I said, meaning it came from the cow our grandfather owned.

I hoped Brown Sugar would someday replace Big Mama when she died, and my grandfather's ties to the farm would continue in Brown Sugar. But I understood where my father was coming from. It was a business decision. We would be investing another year in a young heifer that hadn't produced. Still, I fought for her that day in the driving rain, as water dripped off the bills of our caps and ran down our backs.

"But that's Pap's calf," I said again, as if he truly owned her beyond the grave.

"She's a runt, Robbie," he said, not looking at me.

The rain fell between us and on us, pelting the manure in the field. He kept shaking the pot of pellets, luring the calves he wanted to sell.

I turned and walked off, saying over my shoulder, "You don't need me."

I always take my toys and go home, so to speak, to get him to relent and see things my way. He doesn't have the wind and stamina to do much these days. He knows this. And calls after me.

He said, "We're not going to do this today. We only fight when we sell the cows. So, get back over here and let's do what needs to be done."

I stopped and turned to face him.

He looked at me and said, "Come on."

Usually, he yelled, and I yelled louder. Then he'd top that, then I'd scream and start throwing things at him. We usually handled selling the cows in this way, because I think deep down, I felt guilty and resentful, where he had learned to bury it deep within him. Farmers must create distance. And I resented him for this and held him responsible for this side of the farm—the business side. But I wonder if my resentment comes from a deeper well. One I've created my own distance from.

People hear us voice our concerns about raising beef cattle and tell us we should be dairy farmers. But what happens to the calves on a dairy farm. See? It's a dirty business all the way around for an animal lover. And we were told not to name the cows. It would help us create emotional distance. But you can't enjoy farm life at a distance. You must be willing to remain open to the love and suffering of a farm. You must be vulnerable to enjoy a relationship with the cows. And it hurts when the mama cows begin their bawling the day after we sell their babies. Their bawls pass over the farm. The wind carries their sadness through the trees.

I know there's a climate concern. I know livestock account for an estimated 14 percent of greenhouse gas. I get it. But cows are animals, too. So, here's the choice: cows or no cows. Will they be sent to a zoo, a reservation, a sanctuary? How can they live in the wild? What about a hunting season? Population control? What will be done about aggressive bulls? I'm all for sending them back to the wild, but how?

Jill and I haven't completely worked through this yet. If we could figure out how to have a cow sanctuary, we would. But researchers are now tampering with the archaea microbe and have developed a vaccine against certain gut microbes responsible for producing methane as cows digest their food. Creation has a way of recreating itself. Maybe there's hope on the horizon for our cows.[20] Let's give researchers time.

I have my favorites. Brown Sugar is one of them. And my father didn't challenge me that morning about Brown Sugar. I let her out of the pen and ran her toward the herd.

Soon, we had the calves we wanted in the barn. My father said he was going home to take a hot shower. I waited at the barn for Cowboy Tommy. I was rain-soaked and desired a cup of coffee. And the stockyard had even called to ask if we had gotten the calves up and ready for the hauler. I guess they doubted anybody would really get calves up in that kind of weather. But they didn't know the tenacity of the father and the son.

What Lewis F. Allen said: *In the modern world, among the more highly cultivated classes of society, in polite literature it has been considered vulgar to talk of cattle, or to illustrate them other than as appendages to scenery, landscape, and rural representations among a rude and uncultivated people.*

We had a blind calf our first winter on the farm. She didn't have the usual white eyes of a blind cow. We hardly noticed something was wrong until she became a young heifer. My father always said, "There's something different about that calf." And we'd watch as she kept her distance from the herd, just enough not to get pushed around. They seemed annoyed by her and would head-butt her out of the way. Sometimes she butted them back, but it looked more like she did it by accident, as if she failed to see them coming. Then one day she went headlong over a pile of brush and rolled down a hill, only to get up and hit a tree. We knew after that day. And, luckily, she was okay.

Jill named the blind cow Q-tip. She was brindle with a patch of white at the end of her tail and could follow the herd. By smell, I'm sure. Getting to the pond by smell or by counting her steps. Who knows? But she navigated the farm blind. She walked through the gates and traversed the long pasture without falling into the ditches. She felt her way around. At times, she ran nose first into barbwire, then turned and changed direction. But most of the time she seemed happy and content.

While moving the cows one day, Q-tip went the wrong direction and ended up in a wooded area recently cleared of timber. The tops of trees left on the ground were like tentacles reaching out to trip her up, and she stumbled over limbs and stumps, scraping the hide off her legs. We did our best to get her back in the pasture. One wrong move could've landed her in a deep wood, a place of no return for a blind and wayward cow.

Eventually, she found the fence and her way back to the pasture. She rubbed along the fence like an out of control racecar scrubbing along the wall of a racetrack.

By midsummer of our second year on the farm, Q-tip had seemingly lost the will to follow the herd. Maybe they ostracized her. Maybe it was too much work. Maybe she was exhausted. Tired of trying to fit in. Tired of pasture rotation. Maybe she preferred a wasteland, because she circled a hilltop just above our house. Most days we watched as she made circular motions like a car cruising a town. Round and round she would go. Behind this tree, around another, to the top, to the bottom. Then she'd stop and raise her nose, before starting the same pattern.

Her weight had dropped. Her ribs extruded. We thought about putting her down, but none of us had the heart to shoot her. Jill would go to the hill and talk to her. Q-tip would lift her ears and stop to listen. I'm not sure what she said to Q-tip. It hurt too much to ask. Then the night of the Fourth of July, the small town where we live celebrated with fireworks. That night Q-tip disappeared. We figured the fireworks spooked her, causing her to rush into one of the many deep ravines on the farm, where she couldn't get out. We searched and searched but never found her body. Nothing. It was like she had been raptured. The hill bare and forlorn, only an abandoned salt block.

I called my father the night I got in a fight with the supervisor. My father vowed to get revenge. I was the reason he went after the supervisor. I was the reason my father was arrested and put in jail that night.

I'm the reason Q-tip suffered and disappeared.

The Front Gate

1979

The next Friday night, I maneuvered through the front gate of the football stadium, which was guarded by teachers and booster club volunteers. The crowd cheered a touchdown, as a long line snaked from the concession stand that was built into the back of the stadium. Some craning their necks trying to keep up with the action on the playing field, as the scent of popcorn mingled with the spirit of football in the damp and windy November night. Bare trees swayed in the woods behind the visitor's side stadium. Some of my druggie friends hung-out behind the end zone, leaning against the fence beneath the scoreboard, occupying unwanted space, trying to keep their distance, inhaling the mist that hovered above the playing field.

    I scanned the bleachers on the home side. Shoulder-to-shoulder fans. Another packed house with Franklin and Brentwood represented. The cheerleaders were at the far end, cheering for the student section. I took a deep breath and tried to psych myself. I dreaded walking the length of the stadium. I checked my trucker's wallet with the chain running to my belt. Made sure it wasn't about to fall out. I had on a new pair of jeans without the doodling and without all the cigarette ashes we rubbed into them to washout the deep blue color. I ran my fingers through the layered sides of my hair to make sure it feathered toward the back. Could I trust Jill

The Front Gate

with my heart? I feared it might all be a trick. Maybe the jocks had talked her into dating me so they could do something weird to me. Something that would embarrass me. Put me back in my place.

I felt the stares—every eye on me—picking apart my faults. But when I glanced to the bleachers, I found their eyes on the game. I ducked my head and began the long walk between the stadium and the chain link fence surrounding the football field. Heavy with shadow. A hotdog wrapper struggled in the air like an afflicted sail, lashed by storms. I kept walking and climbed to the top corner of the bleachers. I pulled the collar up on my blue jean jacket to shield the wind. I leaned against the white concrete block wall at the top, and Jill waved and shot me that smile of hers. Made me think she had been watching for me.

At the end of the first half, Jill motioned for me to meet her behind the bleachers at the concession stand. I watched for signs of Brentwood boys ready to jump me in the shadows. I still couldn't accept this new beginning.

"Hey," she said.

I smiled. "Hey."

"I'm thirsty," she said, then she took me by the arm and led me to the concession stand.

We got in line, and she turned and said, "What a game, huh?"

"Yeah." But I had no idea. I'd been watching her.

"You still want to do something after the game?" she asked.

"Sure," I said. "I've planned on it. Got a full tank of gas."

She laughed and said, "Okay, you'll have to wait on me while I meet with the cheerleaders. Also, my mom and dad want to meet you. They are sitting down near the fifty-yard line."

"Okay, I would love to meet them," I said calmly, but it scared me. I'd rarely met anybody's parents before going out on a date. Usually I just blew the horn, like a taxi. I'd let them off in the same fashion. I might wait until the door closed behind them. I might just pull off without looking to see if they made it inside.

"Meet us at the front gate," she said.

After the game, I leaned against the fence near the entrance gate in the shadows, smoking a cigarette, watching for her. When I saw her walking toward me with her parents, I flicked my cigarette into a clump of grass and waved at the plume of smoke. My heart was pounding. I was afraid they wouldn't approve of me because they were older than I pictured. Her father had peppered grey hair. Maybe six-foot three. Her mother was petite and wore a short fur jacket with her hands in the jacket pockets. She looked down at my feet and back to my face. Then smiled. They seemed all put together. A Brentwood family. And Jill introduced us. I didn't want to say too much or too little. I really didn't want to speak. Fearful of my inadequacies.

Jill said, "This is Robbie."

I shook their hands.

Her father said, "What kind of tires do you have on your car?"

"Sir?"

"Do you have good tires on your car?"

"Dad," Jill said. "Stop."

"Well, I don't want you riding in a car without good tires," he said.

"Stop, Sanford," her mother said. "Okay, honey, just be careful and be home by eleven."

"I will," Jill said, grabbing my hand and pulling me toward the entrance gate.

"Nice to meet you, Robbie," her mother said.

"I'll take care of her," I said over my shoulder.

We walked to the Firebird, as cars snaked out of the parking lot and spread into different directions on Hillsboro Road. I unlocked the passenger side door. She slipped into the seat, catching her cheerleading skirt by the hem, making it flow against her body. I shut the door.

We went to a pizza place, but Jill wouldn't eat. I ate alone. She sat watching me eat. I figured she didn't like pizza, so I asked her.

She said, "No, I love pizza."

"Just not Shakey's Pizza?"

"I'm just not hungry," she said.

Later, she told me she didn't eat that night because she thought I'd think she was fat. She's always been sensitive to her weight because her mother monitored what and how much she ate, saying, "You've had a gracious plenty. You need to watch your weight."

I felt like I had bombed on the first date. We didn't talk much that night because I was so shy and felt I had nothing in common with her, and I was shocked when she kept dating me. We even started talking on the phone during the week. I started writing her notes and passed them to her at school. Notes about how much I loved her, about how blessed I was to be dating her, about how I couldn't believe my dreams had come true, about how I wanted to change for her, which fed into her need to rescue me. She kept the notes in a shoebox beneath her bed and has them somewhere in the house to this day. It amazed me that I could write what I was afraid to say to her face, and these notes solidified our relationship. But face-to-face, I remained shy.

What Anne Lamott said: *When God is going to do something wonderful, He or She always starts with a hardship; when God is going to do something amazing, He or She starts with an impossibility.*[21]

Rescuing a Horse

2019

When we moved to the farm and away from where my grandchildren lived in Alabama, I tried to lessen the blow by telling my granddaughter she could have a horse. She rode a horse at a birthday party once and ever since she'd been talking about her love for horses, even checking out books about horses from the library. But it was an empty promise. I didn't have money for a horse and couldn't afford the upkeep. But Jill told me I couldn't promise something and not deliver on the promise. So, when Jill found a horse at a local horse rescue, I relented.

I think Jill wanted the horse more than my granddaughter, because when Jill was in junior high school, her mother told her she could either have a horse or be a cheerleader. Her sister was already a cheerleader, so—against her real desire—Jill chose cheerleading. And it didn't take me long to realize Jill was correcting some mistakes she'd made as a child.

The first week we got the horse, Jill had him tied in the barnyard with a long lead rope when my father drove up to the gate. When Jill went to open the gate for my father, the horse somehow got spooked by stepping on the lead rope and got the lead rope caught around its back leg. Maybe he thought it was a snake. Who knows? But he started kicking, and the harder he kicked, the tighter the rope got coiled around his leg. And Jill started screaming for help. She said she felt so helpless, but before my father could secure his dog and get to her, Jill had somehow calmed the horse. She said she grabbed his halter, and he looked her in the eye and stopped kicking. Then she unhooked him. But the horse had a deep rope burn on its leg. Jill told me later that she just knew he'd broken his leg and would have to be put down on the spot. But even though it rubbed all the hide from his leg, he seemed okay. Still, Jill took it hard, as if she should've been a better horse owner.

"I failed to protect him," she said, almost in tears. She was shaking allover just telling me about it.

Later that night, I was downstairs watching the news when I heard crying upstairs. I found Jill in the bathtub sobbing. Really blubbering. Her hands over her face.

I said, "Tell me what's going on."

"It was awful. I just knew he was going to break his leg. I'm so dumb. Something told me to untie him before I opened the gate for your father, but I just ignored it. Why did God let that happen? We were having such a great day. I've never been happier, and then just out of the blue, it happened. I wanted to keep him safe and offer him a happy home, then that had to happen. I pray for protection all the time. I lie awake at night in bed and just pray and pray, because whenever things are going good, something bad always has to happen. This has happened my whole life."

I said, "But he's fine. He's going to be okay. He'll heal up."

She put her hands over her face and cried.

I didn't know the depth of her tenderness until we moved to the farm and worked with animals. Sure, I knew she had a tender heart toward her children and me, but this discovery of tenderness toward animals helped me understand what her family may have missed by allowing her to become a cheerleader like her sister. She always paled when trying to match her sister's goodness. Her sister had a natural goodness, almost otherworldly. She was the most popular girl at Franklin High School and died of cancer as a young woman—following her mother's own bout with cancer.

The following day, Jill picked up a cassette that I had placed on one of the bedroom dressers after cleaning out my office. It was labeled "Patti Whitehurst." It was her mother's testimony near the end of her life. She spoke at a Tuesday morning Bible study that met at the Whitehurst house at the time, and someone had taped it.

Jill stuck her head in my home office and wanted to know if I could get the cassette to play in an old CD/Cassette boombox. I did. I hadn't heard her mother's voice in twenty years. She sounded weak and frail yet determined to deliver her message about cancer and the body of Christ. Jill cried some more, then halfway through the tape, she shut it off and went back to the barn. I didn't ask her why she hadn't finished the tape. Maybe she just needed to hear her mother's voice.

What Henri Nouwen said: *Still, as long as you keep pointing to the specifics, you will miss the full meaning of your pain.*[22]

The Town Square

1979

One night after a basketball game, I asked Jill, "Where do you want to go?"

"Let's ride around Franklin."

We'd talked about life on the streets in Franklin when we talked on the phone. But this was the first time she wanted to enter my world at street level.

"It'll probably bore you."

"Maybe not," she said.

"Okay, don't say I didn't warn you."

I started the Firebird.

"Wait. Let me get out of this uniform."

She reached for a duffle bag she'd brought with her and pulled out a pair of Levi jeans. She reached down and removed whatever she had on beneath the skirt. Her legs were golden. Then she worked the jeans up over her hips. She looked over at me with her green eyes and said, "Turn your head."

I laughed and did so. Transfixed and glowing.

"Okay," she said.

When I turned to look at her, she had on a T-shirt. The cheerleading uniform with the massive letters FHS for Franklin High School lay in her lap. She bent down and pulled on a pair of chestnut-colored moccasins. Her brown feathered-Farrah-Fawcett-hair hung down her chest. "Okay, ready," she said with a little sigh.

We turned out of the school parking lot and she reached for the radio and turned it up, saying, "Hey, I love this song!"

I lit a cigarette, holding the wheel straight with my knee. I cracked the window. Took a draw off the cigarette, and then exhaled it. I slumped in the seat and tried to loosen up, as we circled the town square and waved at the usual cast of characters that hung out there.

When the song ended, she echoed what she said at the beginning, "I love that song."

I smiled before taking a drag off my cigarette.

"Who did you just wave at back there at the liquor store?"

"At the liquor store?"

"Yeah, you just waved at a guy back there." She turned and looked back. "The guy with the hat."

"It was probably James Brown." I wasn't paying much attention when I waved, but knew James was a permanent fixture at the liquor store and usually wore a hat.

"Stop messing with me. Who is it, really?"

"I'm not kidding," I said with a laugh. "His name is James Brown."

"No, it's not."

"Yes, it is. You want to go ask him?" I didn't actually think she would take me up on it.

"Okay, let's do it. I want to meet a guy named James Brown." She gave me the sweetest smile. A smile I'd seen at football games as the cheerleaders tumbled onto the field at halftime.

Suddenly she made all of my routine movements of cruising town feel awkward. I noticed the slow rhythm of the blinker. I felt the roar of the gears inside the transmission when I downshifted to first gear, the way the Hood's Liquor Store sign illuminated the faces of the men hanging around outside the store, and the way they fidgeted around as they talked and bobbed their heads.

James removed a hand from his jacket pocket and held up a finger to the guy he was talking with and approached the passenger side window that Jill had rolled down.

"What's up, my man?" James said.

"Nothing much," I said.

He looked Jill over and said, "Now who is this fine-looking girl you got with you?"

"This fine-looking girl wants to ask you something." I said, opening the invitation for Jill's question.

"Now what you got to ask me, baby?"

"What's your name?"

"My name?"

"Yeah."

"Baby, my name is James Brown."

"See, I told you." I looked out at James. "She didn't believe me when I told her your name."

"Well, baby, I'm the original James Brown. That other dude is ugly as hell and got those nasty scars all over his face. He ain't got nothing on this face, baby." He ran his hand over his face as if he'd just finished shaving and was checking the smoothness of the shave. "So, what's your name?"

Jill stopped laughing and said, "Jill . . . Jill Whitehurst."

"Well, Jill, it's nice to meet you." James held out his hand and Jill shook it. "Now what are y'all smoking in here tonight? Got any weed?"

It embarrassed me. I didn't want Jill to know this, so I just laughed and said, "Can you buy me something to drink?"

"Y'all want something?"

"Yeah," Jill said.

"What you want, baby?"

"What do you recommend?" Jill said.

"Tonight, I'm drinking some Screwdriver, which is a little bit of vodka in orange juice. What about that?"

"Okay," she said. Then she looked at me. "Does that sound good? Would you drink some?"

I dug into the front pocket of my jeans and pulled out a twenty I'd stolen from the cash register at the auto parts store that afternoon, and then passed it to him. "Here's some money, James."

James took it and headed inside the store. I knew he'd return and want a joint for his services.

I hoped I wasn't getting her mixed up in my craziness. I shifted around in the seat and grabbed my collection of cassettes out of the backseat. "What do you want to listen to?"

"Let me see what you have?"

I passed the collection to her and she pulled out Boston. I put it in the tape deck and Boston's mesmerizing guitar riffs began about the time James Brown returned with the fifth of Screwdriver in a brown paper bag.

James handed Jill the fifth and said, "All right, my man, whatcha got for me?"

I had no choice. I opened the glove box, pulled out a plastic sandwich bag, and unrolled it, exposing ten perfectly rolled joints. I'd taken my time with them, clearing out the seeds and rolling them up into tight sticks with just the right amount of spit. I dug one out and passed it on to James.

He looked around and stuck it in his mouth. "Y'all want to smoke it with me?" James said, lighting it.

"Naw, man, we got a party to go to."

"Yeah, I know. I see that party. Yes, sir. I see it." He took a long toke. Held it.

I shot him a peace sign.

He held up a fist.

I put the Firebird into gear and refocused my vision through the windshield. We slipped back into the traffic.

"Let's head out of town and go down some backroads. It'll be safer than riding around town with open alcohol," I said.

"Okay," she said with one hand holding the fifth, the other one holding my hand on the console.

This felt so good. So right. And once we cleared the city limits, she twisted the top off and took a long drink with the bottle still inside the brown bag. The paper crackled as she turned up the bottle. "This stuff isn't too bad. Kind of tastes like orange Kool-Aid. Try it."

She took another drink, then passed me the bottle.

"I know where a party is," she said, turning to me, watching the way I smoked my cigarette.

I wondered what kind of party it might be. Brentwood boys were on a different wavelength than us Franklin boys. But I followed her directions to some party in the hills of Brentwood. She reached for the bottle and took a drink.

"I've changed my mind. Turn here!" she said.

I cut the wheel and took a hard-left turn.

"Where are we going?" I said.

"Have you ever been to Percy Warner Park?"

I couldn't believe the question. I shifted to fourth gear and said, "Yeah, all the time."

"Cool. Let's go there." She pushed the eject button of the stereo, removing Boston. She put the tape in the collection and chose Journey. She pushed it into the tape deck.

"Do you go to the park on Sundays?" I asked.

"Yeah. I love Sundays in the park."

How many times had we seen one another unaware? My friends and I threw Frisbee there most every Sunday during the summer.

"Oh! I know where to go," she said suddenly. Leaning toward me. "Have you ever been to where gravity pulls your car up the hill?"

"Where?"

"You know, that hill where gravity pulls you back up the hill."

"Oh, yeah. That place," I said happy to find some common experience outside school stuff. "It's freaky. It's like someone is pulling you back up the hill."

I'd never been there at night. The park was asleep beneath a layer of fog. I hit the high beams and followed the narrow road that led through the park. We traveled over hills and around sharp turns without guardrails. Deep woods on both sides of the narrow road.

"Don't you love this place? It makes you feel like we are driving into haunted woods," she said.

I smiled, and she reached and opened the glove box, drawing out the bag of weed. She opened it and stuck one between my lips. She reached for the lighter I'd used to light a cigarette and flicked it. Then she put the flame to the end of the joint. I took a long draw. The end of the joint glowed. She took it from my mouth and smoked it like a cigar, never inhaling. Then handed it back, saying, "That's nasty."

I was glad she hated it.

When we reached *gravity hill*, she leaned up on the dashboard and said, "Okay, stop. Now put it in neutral."

I followed her instructions as if it were my first time.

She turned the radio off and rolled down her window. I followed her lead.

Nature floated through the windows as smoke wafted out. Crickets were chirping. A bird fluttered from a nearby tree. A siren wailed in the distance, as we sat in this haven just outside Nashville.

"Feel it!" she said in a whisper, as if her voice might scare away whatever force pulled cars up the hill.

It was a snail's pace, but we were definitely rolling back up the hill. It was a freaky feeling that I enjoyed.

"See, I told you," she said, elbowing me.

I smiled and applied my foot to the brake. I leaned over, she met me between the bucket seats, and we kissed.

When we emerged from the dark county road, we slipped beneath the streetlights in front of Rebel Meadows subdivision. We drove around another hour, until the fifth of screwdriver was empty. We had settled into a conversation about her family, about how I live with my father, about the auto parts store, and about the time I saw her riding in the Franklin Rodeo parade as the reigning Franklin Rodeo Queen.

She laughed. "Oh, my," she said.

"You waved at me," I said.

"I waved at everyone," she said with a laugh.

The Bottom of the Bottle

1980

What Gerald May said: *I am now becoming dependent upon it, needing it, and wanting more and more of it. This is the beginning of tolerance.*[23]

Basketball season ended. Graduation was two weeks away. The days were getting warmer. And to the surprise of many, Jill and I were still dating. We talked on the phone most every night. Our school had a two-track system that separated "college-bound" students from "vocational" students. In the afternoon, I went to vocational school and studied auto repair. In the mornings, I had remedial classes and rarely saw Jill, especially if I went outside between classes and smoked a cigarette behind the yellow line.

We dated on the weekends. And one weekend, we had James Brown buy us Screwdriver again, and once we finished the bottle, we had him buy another one. And we circled Franklin and drove through the countryside—out past cows and across train tracks without warning signals, out to where light pollution loses its stain on the Milky Way. The windows were down. Heat rose through the floorboards from the engine and transmission. A muscle car is an oven without A/C. So, we drank more than we should have. We drank and talked and laughed. We listened to one cassette, then another—Journey, Boston, Loverboy, REO Speedwagon, even Chicago. Jill liked the horns. She told me of how her mother would make her brother practice his trumpet out in their Cadillac in the driveway. She said his trumpet about drove her mother crazy. I loved hearing about her family, about how her brother set the doghouse on fire while playing with matches. Now he was on his way to play football at Alabama.

She wanted to know about my work at my father's auto parts store. I told her I delivered parts mainly. I didn't tell her I dusted shelves, swept the parking lot and emptied the trash. I made it sound like I was the fastest delivery boy in town, like that would impress her.

I reached for my Bob Seger cassette out of habit. *Live Bullet* was how Coconut and I always ended our night cruising town. Maybe I should have realized before that moment that Jill had grown quiet. But I was in the usual groove. Coconut and I did this most every night. We smoked ten joints a day. More on the weekend. Plus, all the pills—PCP, acid, Quaaludes, amphetamines, and on rare occasions cocaine. I had no reason to believe we were headed for trouble.

I asked at one point, "Are you okay?"

Jill answered with crazy gibberish. I worried she might be too drunk to take home.

I pulled over to get the bottle away from her, to talk some sense into her. But before I could say anything, she opened the door of the Firebird and stumbled out. She fell into the ditch in front of someone's house.

I got out. I went around to the front of the car—the smell of the radiator—the sound of belts turning—laughter. She was on her back in the ditch, laughing up at the moon. The blinker flashed in her face. Her breath waxed and waned.

"Come on Jill, let's get back in the car."

"Nuh-uh."

"Now come on . . . Get back in the car before the police see us. Come on, I'll help you."

I retrieved her from the ditch and took the bottle away from her. I got her back in the Firebird about the time a car approached from behind. I kept one eye on her and the other eye on the car in the rearview mirror. I hoped it wasn't the police. But the car didn't slow. We were safe. I turned around in the road. The front-end of the Firebird popped and creaked. I kept cranking on the wheel to keep it out of the ditch on the other side. Jill was quiet. I could see the passing car's taillights crawling toward the edge of the neighborhood in my rearview mirror. She propped her arm against the door, the other hand resting in her lap.

I pulled to a stop at the red-light across the street from the high school. I needed time to think. I could see the double doors that led into the gymnasium where she cheered. Cars passed in front of us. A red, four door Buick the color of Boone's Farm Strawberry wine. A white Ford one-ton pick-up with a dog standing on a toolbox in the back. It blew its horn. The dog barked. A motorcycle passed.

We sat under the glow of the red-light. The light splashed into the cab creating an erroneous feeling of fire. I was worried about her. I didn't know what to do. I knew my father was out of town. Maybe I could get things under control there. I had to get Jill sober. This was a first for me. I'd never had this happen on a date. The girls I usually dated held their liquor better than I did.

The light turned green. I steered the Firebird steadily across town, checking the rearview mirror for the police. Paranoia always kept my eyes on what surrounded me. I passed the Sonic Drive-in, Williamson County Bank, Kroger. Then I turned left into my father's neighborhood—a neighborhood that had once been the newest subdivision in town. Now it was rundown and cluttered with junk cars, oil spots, rusty-bent swing sets. I turned into the driveway. The muffler drug the pavement as I gunned it up the slope to my father's house.

I sat stunned—beating myself up for not taking better care of her—as the Firebird's engine ticked toward cool. The light of the neighbor's kitchen cast a square in the dark yard.

I rounded the car. I opened the passenger door.

"Where are we?" she asked.

"We're at my father's house. Are you feeling okay?"

"Not really."

"Yeah, let me help you out."

She didn't refuse. She leaned on me. I led her as she shuffled her feet up the concrete driveway. We climbed onto the porch. I steadied her balance.

"Lean against this column while I find my key."

I looked around to see if neighbors were watching. I couldn't tell. I turned the key and unlocked the door. It was hot inside. I fumbled with the light switch. The light spilled onto the porch as I gathered her in my arms and walked across the living room. I placed her on the couch in front of the console RCA television and reached to turn it on. Noise couldn't hurt. A little something to keep us attached to a sane world.

Some man selling exercise equipment appeared on the screen, talking about four easy installments. I went to turn on the air and heard her throwing up in the living room.

I ran back to her and held her hair out of her face. I feared alcohol poisoning. I knew of a guy who let his girlfriend die. She had too much to drink at a keg party one night, and he sneaked her into her house and put her to bed. The next morning her mother found her dead, and I thought Jill might die. I retrieved cold washcloths for the back of her neck. I couldn't think. Did not want to think about what was happening. *Maybe she'll get better. Maybe she just needs to get the Screwdriver out of her system.* Then I noticed she was looking blue or green. I couldn't tell. I propped her up on the couch. She fell back over the edge and started the whole process again. So, I had to end it somehow . . . right?

"Mrs. Whitehurst, uh . . . this is Robbie . . . and—"

"What's wrong?"

The Probability of a Pierced Heart

1980

I told Mrs. Whitehurst, "Well, Jill is not feeling good. She's sick."
"Is she sick at her stomach or what?"
"Yes ma'am, sick at her stomach."
"Was it something she ate?"
"Something she drank."
"What has she been drinking?"
"I'm afraid she might have alcohol poisoning."
As soon as I gave her directions, the line went dead.

Her mother never said for me to call 911. I don't think she realized Jill's condition or maybe I was just in a panic.

I waited for her to make the twenty-minute drive from Brentwood, hoping she'd know what to do next. I kept Jill off her back, her airways clear. I remembered Jimi Hendrix's death. I thought about Bon Scott's, the lead singer of AC/DC.

Finally, the doorbell rang. I opened the door. Jill's mother and sister stood on the porch. Her mother looked as though she'd been in bed asleep. Her hair was unkempt. Gone was the put together look, gone was the fresh face and easy mannerisms, and Jill's sister had on thick glasses she never wore at school.

"Hey," I said in a weak, shy voice.

"Where is she?" Her mother demanded.

"She's in here on the couch."

Her mother stormed past me. "Jill, honey, are you okay? How much did you have to drink?"

"I can't remember," she said.

"About a fifth of Screwdriver," I offered.

Her mother shot me a look of disdain and helped Jill to her feet. Her sister grabbed the other arm. They led her to the bathroom. Jill hung over the commode.

"Stick your finger down your throat," her mother insisted.

"Mom, there's nothing left."

"Just do it!"

Jill tried. She heaved. I couldn't tell if anything came up. It sounded like dry heaves.

"Did he give you drugs?"

"No ma'am. I'd never take drugs. I promise. Don't be mad."

Jill's mother said, "It just surprises me, Jill. I never thought you'd do something stupid like this."

Her mother looked at me and said, "I knew something like this was going to happen. I should have never trusted you with Jill. I had this check in my spirit the first time I met you, but I gave you the benefit of the doubt."

I didn't know what a *check in her spirit* meant, but I said, "I'm sorry, Mrs. Whitehurst. I didn't know she was getting this drunk."

"This drunk?!"

I went outside and circled the house. The stars were bent over the roof, the wind tossed the trees. My heart pounded for love and escape. But I knew I had to go back inside. I had to face something I knew better than to let happen. I felt it would be the last time I'd ever see Jill. Her parents were smart. They'd keep her away from me.

Jill's mother led her from the house and onto the front porch where I stood. I dug my hands deep into my pockets and slumped my shoulders. Preparing myself for the tongue-lashing.

"I'm sorry," I said, as they reached the door.

Jill looked up. "It's not your fault."

The Probability of a Pierced Heart

"Both of you played a part in this. We better be glad you didn't die," her mother said.

I stepped aside. They worked their way down the driveway. I followed and kept offering excuses, lying about Jill's involvement. "It wasn't Jill's fault, Mrs. Whitehurst. I talked her into it. You got to believe me. I'll never let this happen again, though. I promise."

Her sister pushed me back when I tried to help. Her elbow prodded me.

Her sister shut the door, enclosing Jill inside. Then her mother walked to me standing on the curb and said, "Never again will you take my daughter out on a date. Don't call our house. Don't even speak to her in public. Her father is six foot-three. Tonight, he's out of town, and if you try to contact Jill, you will hear from him." Then she stomped off.

I didn't respond, only looked to where Jill sat in the car. She waved and mouthed the words, "I'm sorry." I waved back with one hand in my pocket and a hollow, sinking feeling in my gut. I ran my fingers through my hair as the green Cadillac maneuvered out of my father's driveway and disappeared over the hill in the neighborhood.

I went back inside to clean the place up. The smell hit me when I opened the door.

What George Armatage said: *Cattle are peculiarly disposed to pick up and swallow very strange articles. When these comprise sharp or pointed instruments, as needles, pins, skewers, etc., the natural motions of the stomach cause them to enter the walls and pass onwards, until in all probability the heart is pierced.*[24]

A Longing for Hope

1980

Most nights I couldn't sleep after being banned from seeing Jill. I stared at the ceiling and listened to WKDF, the rock station out of Nashville. I drove around Franklin with Coconut, who tried to keep me sane and occupied. I wasn't sure how to get Jill back. I feared her parents. Maybe Jill's mother was right, and I believed her and stayed away from Jill. I'd hurt someone I loved, so maybe I was all wrong for her. And I started hitting the drugs heavier. I punished myself. I was good at this.

The year after my mother left, I started junior high school and used Principle Brown to punish me on a weekly basis. I did things that got me sent to his office. He wouldn't send me back to class until he'd administered five licks with his paddle that had holes drilled in it. Once, I forgot to take a pack of rolling papers out of my back pocket. At the time, I was smoking a joint before the 7th grade each morning. Thankfully he hadn't noticed the square and hadn't said, "Empty your pockets." I had a red square on my behind for a few days, the perfect shape of the pack of rolling papers.

Winded after administering the five licks, I could smell cigarette smoke on Principle Brown's breath. At some point, he stopped lecturing me. He just handed me a hall pass and pointed to the door. He never suspended me because I think he liked the punishment as much as I did. He put his anger in the swing, and I took it like a man. (Today, I have Ischial bursitis, which is basically a *pain in the butt*. I wonder if it's from all the licks with a paddle.)

I started this punishment again after being banned from Jill. I did crazy things that resembled the behavior of the adolescents I had in my writing class at the psych hospital. I understood why it got so dark for my uncles. I can remember this kid once that was admitted to the psych hospital where I worked. Both of his eyes were black and blue. I asked the nurse what happened to him, and she said, "The little dummy beat himself up." I understood and tried to befriend the boy. For I had blacked both of my eyes once.

At the auto parts store, I couldn't focus when I answered the phone. A mechanic would give me the make and model of a car, and I would open the catalog on the counter, then forget and would have to ask again. My father noticed and told me if I couldn't remember, then to at least write it down. Mechanics even started asking for my father when I answered the phone. I missed being at school. I'd always wanted the freedom of being at the auto parts store every day, but it was boring. Meaningless. Not what I thought adulthood would feel like.

I did a hit of acid one night and prayed to God for the first time. I don't recommend this as your first encounter. I'd never spoken to Him before in my life. But I knew if I was going to get Jill Whitehurst back, then I needed some higher power. I needed a connection with someone greater than her mother. But I didn't know a Christian, a monk, or a street preacher. I had no mentor. I don't remember praying as a child. No one ever said, "Let's pray." No one suggested we call the pastor and have him pray. We didn't know a pastor or a priest. We knew nothing of prayer chains. We hoped instead of prayed. We hoped we wouldn't get lockjaw from a rusty nail that punctured the bottoms of our Converse tennis shoes. We hoped we wouldn't grow up and be sterile as my mother said we would be if we kept smoking Marlboro Reds. We hoped it wouldn't rain on Sundays, so we could motocross race. We hoped the way most people prayed. We just hoped the sun would rise. We just hoped we would have enough money to buy more weed and pills. If we didn't, I stole money out of my father's cash register.

Then we hoped he wouldn't notice. If he did, he never mentioned it.

So, with the effects of acid still in my brain, I prayed. "God, I'll stop doing drugs and everything, if you'll give Jill Whitehurst back."

I figured God would jump at the deal. You know, the old, "You scratch my back, and I'll scratch yours." I figured this was how spirituality worked—tit-for-tat. To get God to do something, you had to promise to quit committing some sin. I mean, what did I have to lose? Either He would answer, or He would continue to care for more important world issues. It was a selfish prayer.

What M. Scott Peck said: *The path to holiness lies through questioning everything.*[25]

What George A. Buttrick said: *"We walk the path, whatever our chosen path, for we cannot wait for explanations. Pain is not a theory but a daily onset."*[26]

Graduation

1980

Graduation was held at the Franklin High football stadium. It was my first time to step on to the football field. We sat in folding chairs spread out in rows in front of a makeshift stage. The stadium lights were like the lights of an OR. That night they cut adolescence from our bones and spread the future before us like a recovery room, where we would all eventually wake up in the *real world* with various pains and paths into the land of fulfillment. Coconut and I were pushed through the system as good riddance. Our grades were lousy. We were at the bottom of our class. We didn't care. But at least they were kind enough to graduate us.

Things started falling apart after graduation. I no longer had the right to be at school. I was no longer a child. I had to put childish ways behind me.

If I walked across the stage at graduation and shook the principle's hand, I have no recollection of it. I don't remember his cold or moist hand in mine. I don't remember taking the diploma with the other hand, even though I know it happened because the diploma hangs on the wall in my office. I'd taken speed, which always increased my paranoia. This I remember. Later, I remember being alone at a party and drinking PGA in grape Kool-Aid. The following Monday, I went to work delivering parts and stocking shelves, knowing Jill had one more year at Franklin High without me.

Clippings

1980

I missed being at school. I'd always dreamed of the freedom to be at the auto parts store every day, but it was boring. I could only think about school and about the pep rallies I was missing. I wondered if Jill had made the cheerleading squad. I thought about going to the games, but I felt barred from that old life. I didn't want a face-to-face happenchance with Jill's parents, so I longed for some miracle encounter with Jill out on the streets of Franklin as I delivered auto parts. I jumped for every delivery that crossed the counter. Maybe I would see her mother's green Cadillac in Franklin, instead of Brentwood. It was a longshot. But I had no other course of action. And I felt God had probably abandoned me as well since I hadn't quit doing drugs either.

Joe Ennis, one of the only black mechanics, whom I loved very much, ordered an alternator for Mrs. Gray's '72 Chevy Nova. Badfinger—we called him this because he lost a finger while working on an engine—wrote up the ticket. I jumped into delivery truck and headed down Church Street, around the town square, down past the Suzuki shop—headed to Joe's garage that was just before you got to Harlinsdale Farms. I pulled into the parking lot. Slid the truck to a stop and grabbed Joe's alternator off the seat. I rounded the corner of his shop and noticed Franklin's local newspaper, *The*

Review Appeal, sitting on his desk. It was open to the section that pictured Franklin High's homecoming queen. Jill stood by her father. She was entering her limelight. Her sister had always left her in the shadows. Her sister was a beloved cheerleader and leader of popularity, overshadowing Jill. But now the attention had turned to her. She was the most popular one. She won homecoming queen and would go on to be voted *Most Outstanding Senior*. She was beautiful under the stadium lights. I'll never forget that picture. She looked happy, which made me sad. I missed her. I gazed at her. Kept gazing. Gazed some more. Then Joe stepped around the corner and spoke.

"That was fast," he said.

"Yes, sir, I'm taking care of you," I said, extending the alternator in his direction.

He smiled and sat the alternator on the desk.

I handed him the ticket.

He looked at it. Folded it and dug in his pocket. He fished out a wad of dollar bills and peeled them off.

I gave him change.

"Joe, you mind if I have this section of the paper?"

"I don't see why not. What interests you in that section?"

I blushed and said, "A girl."

"Oh! A girl. Well, by all means, take it."

"Thanks, Joe."

He smiled and put the wad of bills back in the pocket of his blue coveralls that had *Joe* over one pocket and *Ennis Repair* over the other one.

When I got back to the auto parts store, I cut the picture out using the Buck knife I carried in a leather case on my hip. I took it home and taped it next to the other picture above my bed. I felt close to her. I know that sounds sappy. But it was the truth. I stared at her for hours at a time. I would rush home after work and sit in my room with AC/DC blaring in my stereo. I'd sit and stare at her picture and wonder what she was doing.

What William Robertson Nicoll said: *We may try to stifle the hideous fear that looms out from dark places of the heart, till it grows impossible. But if we face the truth and accept it with steady, tender, patient submission, some better thing will come.*[27]

Back in the Saddle

1981

The football team had racked up another losing effort. Now basketball season had started and Coconut wanted to attend a game. He picked out his afro in front of the bathroom mirror at the supervisor's house while I listened to his argument about why we should go to the game that night.

I said, "It makes you look like a loser to attend a basketball game after you've graduated."

"You are already a loser, so get over it. Marla and her friends are going to be there. Maybe you'll like one of them," he said. "You need to think about moving on."

Truth be told, I felt like I had a restraining order taken out against me. This was probably what her parents wanted me to feel. But I could tell Coconut wanted to go. The social butterfly needed interaction.

"What if Jill's mother is there?" I said.

Coconut said, "Look, they don't own the school. We go and act like everything is cool."

The high school parking lot was full for the Tuesday night game. There were no spots on the pavement. So, I parked out beside the football stadium in the grass. We got out and met at the front of the Firebird. Coconut grabbed my blue jean jacket collar and said, "Look at me. You are the man, you hear me? Go in there and act like you have moved on."

I laughed and said, "Okay."

He said, "Women don't like needy guys."

"I'm definitely that," I said with a laugh.

Cold air pushed us through the door and into the lobby. The double doors to the gym were open, and I could see the cheerleaders at the far end. Their arms in constant motion. I spotted Jill. The hurt rushed through me.

The gym had a sweaty smell. Coconut and I climbed to the top of the bleachers. Climbed to where a window was open, to where heat met cold air. We watched from this vantage point. It seemed like a year since I'd seen her. I'd forgotten her mannerisms. The way she moved. The way she smiled and laughed. I scanned the gym for her mother. Once I found her, I quickly looked away and felt my face flush.

It brought back those same feelings the last time I saw her, as she maneuvered the green Cadillac out of my father's driveway and traversed the neighborhood. Her taillights glowing at the end of the street.

At halftime, Coconut and I followed everyone into the lobby, where we hung-out in the crowd. I looked over to where Jill stood with two other cheerleaders. I wanted to see if I could catch her eye. Maybe I could interpret the look. Maybe not. Somehow, I felt she held me accountable for what happened that night or maybe she was the kind of girl that just honored her parents' wishes, which was foreign to me.

I finally caught her eye.

She smiled.

Coconut said, "I'll go talk to her."

I grabbed him at first, then released him with a nod. I didn't want to do anything to get her in further trouble with her parents.

At the beginning of the third period, Coconut climbed the bleachers where I sat and said, "Her parents grounded her indefinitely, so you must've really pissed them off."

My throat tightened.

Back in the Saddle

"But there is good news," he said. "She started working at Mr. Gatti's Pizza."

Mr. Gatti's Pizza was a new franchise in Franklin. The first to have a big screen television, and people would go eat pizza and gawk at it. The television offered a new dining atmosphere in a town mostly known for meat and three restaurants. A Wendy's and a McDonald's had just opened a few years before Mr. Gatti's. For the first few weeks McDonalds was open, I ate a Big Mac every day, surrounded by pictures and sayings of Benjamin Franklin. Why McDonalds chose this interior decoration, I'll never know. But McDonalds paved the way for other franchises.

"Ok, and why is that good?"

"Well, she told me to tell you to drop by and see her," Coconut said, putting his arm around me. He was the only one I let embrace me. "Yep. You're back in the saddle. Don't mess it up." Then he started singing the Aerosmith song. "Back in the saddle again. I'm baaack." Then he laughed, throwing his head back.

Coconut always mixed song lyrics into what he said, and he was the only one that could make it sound natural and cool.

Mr. Gatti's

1981

Mr. Gatti's sat at the bottom of a small incline. Surrounded by a Kroger grocery store and a Wendy's. Jill stood behind the counter taking orders when I walked through the door. She was wearing a newsboy cap and a nerdy uniform with a nametag. I was third in line behind an older couple and a family with a baby. When she smiled at me, it eased my nerves. The menu had been painted on a piece of plywood hanging above her. I studied it while she waited on the ones before me. She took cash and gave back their change. She fixed drinks. She kept smiling at me as she worked.

I wasn't hungry. My gut burned with brimstone and fire.

When it was my turn, she said, "Hello, my name is Jill. Can I take your order?"

It was so sexy the way she said it. I wanted to say, "I'll take you," but thought twice about it when that little voice inside my head screamed, "Don't do it. It's corny."

"How you are doing?" I said.

"I'm okay. How about you?"

"Good. I'm good."

The door behind me opened and a family with loud kids entered. Both of us looked at them. I felt pressured to order, even though I wasn't hungry.

"Let me have a small pepperoni."

"You want a drink?"

"Yeah, I'll take a Coke."

"Okay, I'll bring it to you. We'll talk some more."

I sat at a table and admired the big screen television. It helped settle my nerves.

Ten minutes later, Jill brought the pizza and sat down beside me.

"Hope you're hungry."

"Wow. Thanks." I said.

Instead of a small, it was a large.

"I'm on break, so I can talk for a minute."

"That's good."

"So, you mad at me?" I said, still feeling insecure.

"Me, mad at you? I should be the one asking that question. You didn't pour it down my throat."

"Well, I didn't stop you from pouring it down your throat."

"I was pretty sick, huh?"

"I'd say."

"What did your father say about me throwing up all over his house."

"You threw up all over his house?"

She smirked.

"I'm a good cleaner. I had plenty of time to get the place back in shape."

"You're sweet," she said.

I had never had a girl say that to me. I felt my face blush.

"I'm sorry I called your mother, but it scared me," I said. "I didn't know anybody else to call. I heard you were grounded indefinitely."

"I think she's more disappointed than mad."

I wasn't sure how to navigate disappointment. I knew anger. I've made my parents mad, but disappointment would mean love had something to do with it. I didn't know how to respond.

We stared at one another a second.

"You're not eating," she said.

I grabbed a piece and took a bite.

"You made this?"

"What do you think?" she said, smiling.

"Best pizza I've ever had."

"You better say that."

The father of the loud children approached the table.

"Could you change the channel?" he said to Jill.

"I don't know how, but I'll be happy to get the manager," she said in a syrupy sweet voice.

"Thanks. Tell him my children want to watch *Dukes of Hazard*."

"Okay."

The man turned and went back to his family.

"Meet me after work," she said.

"Okay, but I don't want to get you in trouble."

"You've already done that," she said, laughing.

"What time?"

"Eleven. I'll tell my parents I'm closing, which usually takes until two in the morning."

"If you're sure you won't get in trouble."

She stood and said, "Park by the Cadillac. I'll see you then. And you best eat every piece of that." She walked off and looked over her shoulder. "Just kidding. Eat as much as you want."

I watched the *Dukes of Hazard* episode with the loud family, then followed them out when it was over, waving to Jill behind the counter.

Eleven

1981

I parked by her Cadillac at eleven.

Jill tapped on the window, startling me. I was fingering through my cassette tapes, looking for the latest Journey.

"Hey," she said.

I rolled down the window. "Come around. Get in."

She had changed out of her uniform into her Levi jeans and moccasins. I loved her earthiness. She was the most beautiful girl I'd ever known.

I cleared the passenger seat of cassettes.

She opened the door and got in.

"Hey," she said.

"Y'all looked busy."

"Tell me about it. I bet we cooked a hundred pizzas." She looked around at the interior of the car and said, "I've missed you. I've missed being in your car."

"Well, where do you want to go?" I said.

"Anywhere. Just get me away from here."

I cranked the engine and pulled onto the highway. I went through the gears. Then settled back in the seat. I touched her hand and held it. She didn't move it. She didn't take mine either. She only smiled. She seemed tired. She wasn't saying much. We passed the high school on our way out of town, and she turned and looked at it as if it held some kind of message. The moon in the trees created shadows on the parking lot and on the sides of the building. She studied them. Then she turned and looked at me.

"This makes me nervous," she said. "I feel like my mother is following us or something, but I know she's not."

"You have a great relationship with your mom, don't you?"

"She's been through a lot."

"Yeah?" I said, turning down a Journey song.

"She had breast cancer a few years back, but right now she's in remission."

I felt even worse now about involving her mother that night. I wished I'd never called her. Would things be different?

"That's good, right? That she's in remission?" I said.

"It's very good. So the reason I hadn't tried to contact you was because of how guilty I feel. I disappointed her, which is not your fault."

She moved closer and lightly kissed my cheek.

"You would like my mother," she said.

"I'm scared of your mother."

She laughed.

"She's not mad at you anymore. She just doesn't trust you."

"Sometimes I don't trust myself."

"Well, don't give up on her. She might change her mind about you. It scared her that night at your house."

I'd spent my whole life not trusting people, and now I knew what it felt like being on the receiving end of mistrust. I didn't know how to bridge that gap and make her mother trust me.

"Let's go back to gravity hill in the park," Jill said. "Let's roll back in time and start over."

"I'm all for it."

She unzipped her duffle bag and pulled out her Mr. Gatti's hat. She put it on. "Don't you think I look sexy in this?"

I laughed. "Very sexy."

I liked the playful side of her.

Eleven

We floated back up the incline at gravity hill. We kissed. We rode around the park. Up wooded hills and down again. Everything was back to the way it should be. Moonlit pieces of clouds drifted over the park.

Pumping Gas

1981

Right before I had reunited with Jill, my father fired me from the auto parts store. I'd refused to take the trash out. I don't know what I was thinking. I was just mad and disappointed in myself for losing Jill. I didn't care about anything during that time. Then I realized I needed gas for the Firebird. No way was I staying cooped up in the supervisor's house. I belonged in my Firebird on the streets of Franklin.

I asked my father for my job back. He refused. I couldn't believe it. He'd given the boys who'd worked for him numerous chances to redeem their wayward actions. But not me, which turned out to be one of the best things he could've done for my future.

I took a job at the factory where my mother once worked when she met the supervisor. He had since moved on and started his own company, something to do with the pigmentation in Christmas paper. My mother had become a tennis-playing-housewife in the suburbs. So, with the two of them in better places, I slipped into their old haunt. I lasted two weeks. I hid in boxes and slept until someone kicked the box and alerted me that a supervisor was in the area. Two weeks later, I quit. I took a job at a Shell station in a community between Franklin and Brentwood called Grassland. I pumped gas and changed oil. Got paid nothing. Minimum wage.

Pumping Gas

The only benefit was the location. It sat on the edge of the highway that Jill took to and from school each day her senior year of high school. I would sit at the desk or stand pumping gas, watching for the Cadillac to go by. Sometimes she stopped in the afternoon and bought gas. On slow days when the owner, Big Dave was gone, I sat and wrote Jill long notes of love and longing. It was the perfect job for the moment.

What Thomas Merton said, *The real hope is not in something we think we can do, but in God, who is making something good out of it in some way we cannot see. If we can do God's will, we will be helping in this process. But we will not necessarily know all about it beforehand.*[28]

Set Free

1981

On the night of Jill's graduation, her parents set her free. They said she was eighteen and could date me again, if she so desired. And she called and gave me the news.

"Come to graduation," she said.

I stood before them at graduation, the same way I did the night at the football game. Jill handed her diploma to her mother. They tried to smile at us. I was all smiles, which had to scare them. But what can you do? You have to let go of your child at some point. Maybe they discussed it in bed the night before. Maybe they knew Jill was going to college in the fall, and they could no longer control where she went and who she dated. I'm not sure. But it must have been hard for them.

Most everyone knew I was Jill's downfall. Even the vice principle at Franklin High School warned her. He yelled for her across the football field as the graduation ceremony ended. She walked by my side with her graduation cap in hand.

"Jill, wait up," he yelled. "I need to speak with you."

I let her walk back five yards to where the vice principal stood at midfield without me. I wanted nothing to do with the man. When Coconut and I skipped out at lunch to get high, he would hide behind a tree at the edge of the parking lot and jump out from hiding once we'd stopped at the main highway. He'd say, "Where do you boys think you're going?" He did this a couple of times before we changed up our routine and found different ways off school property.

When she returned, she said he wanted her to get back with her old boyfriend. I guess he felt she had a better chance with him. Sure, I could say something about the old boyfriend. But why? He tried to run me over in the front parking lot of the high school once. I jumped to safety.

To this day, the vice principal's condemnation bothers me more than the old boyfriend's action. How could he see my heart? How did he know I was bad news? We had stopped drinking since that horrible night of alcohol poisoning. I'd tamed myself to pills and weed only, but never around Jill. Now, here comes this joker trying to get in our business. But he had no idea I would be writing about him one day and that you would be reading it. I've popped out from behind the tree on him, but he is dead and gone by now. And there's no pleasure in it.

Demoniac

1981

Jill's mother told Jill I had a sex demon. I wasn't sure what that meant, but I laughed. Maybe it was just a ploy to keep her away from me. It didn't work. She was the most beautiful girl I'd ever been with and there was magnetism. Call it a demon. Call it fate. Call it whatever, and once it happened, we couldn't stop. The first time happened at the supervisor's house. The supervisor and my mother were in the Smoky Mountains for a weekend getaway. I was babysitting Pepper, the supervisor's yapping Schnauzer. I'd agreed to watch him because I figured Jill and I could hang-out there for the weekend. We could watch television and eat the steaks the supervisor had in the freezer. He always had steaks and cold beer.

"You sure they're gone," Jill said when we pulled into the driveway.

"Positive," I said, motoring through the house to the garage in the back.

"Wow, this is a weird house. I can't believe the driveway tunnels through the middle of the house."

I smiled in acknowledgment and cut the engine.

"Hang on. I'm gonna raise the garage door so we can hide the car inside to keep the nosy neighbors from gawking and telling my mom."

I parked the car inside and lowered the garage door.

Pepper met us inside the house and began jumping on our legs, excited to see us.

"I'm gonna let him out." I looked down at Pepper. "Come on, boy. Let's go outside."

Pepper took his sweet time as if he knew it would get my goad. I felt like putting a foot to him.

Back inside, Jill was walking around looking at the pictures on the wall.

"Your mother must like wildlife."

"I think my mother married into those. Kind of manly, don't you think?"

"Not really. They're expensive. The artist is famous for wildlife prints."

"You hungry? I could cook a steak on the grill."

"No, I'm good. I ate earlier."

"Well, let me take you on a tour of the house."

My room was over the tunnel. One wall had a large plate glass window that looked like a sliding glass door. There was a façade balcony on the other side of the window. A large curtain covered the window. Above my queen-size bed was a large picture of the signing of the Declaration of Independence. It belonged to the supervisor and could not be removed or replaced. Orders of the supervisor. It hung there as a reminder of the freedom I'd never have living in that house. There was a large closet with folding doors. The oak dresser belonged to the supervisor, unlike the one I had at my father's house that was made of pressed-wood. Nothing about the room resembled my tastes, except the Farrah Fawcett poster.

"This is the weirdest house," Jill said.

"I know. My room is over the driveway. Funny to think about."

Jill went to the window, pulled back the heavy curtain, and peered down at the driveway to get her bearings. Then she turned and spotted the trophies I'd won racing motocross.

"Oh, my gosh. Did you win all of those?"

"Yeah."

I'd never felt prouder of them. I had nothing by the way of accolades at school.

"This one is unique," Jill said, touching it.

It had reflective tape down the sides and the motorcycle on top was doing a wheelie. I'd won it at Andrew Jackson Raceway in Nashville. I loved that track with its smooth berms and sloping hills.

She sat on the bed, facing the dresser looking at the trophies. Then she noticed her picture on the wall by the bed.

She laughed and said, "Where did you get that?"

"Out of the paper," I said, berating myself for forgetting it was there.

"You're such a stalker."

I smiled.

She leaned over and kissed me, then said, "It's strange to think that there's nothing below us holding up the floor."

I laughed. "You can't get that off your mind, can you?"

The thought added weightlessness to the moment, as if we were on a cloud.

"It's just strange, that's all," she said.

"It's the hottest room in the summer and the coldest in the winter."

"I can see how that would be true."

I gently pushed her back on the bed and kissed her.

She said, "You sure your mother is not coming home?"

"She's not. I promise."

Let Me Introduce You

1981

The following week, when my mother came home from their trip, Jill told me she'd like to meet my family, so we drove to the supervisor's house. I had been staying at my father's house a couple of nights and hadn't seen my mother since dog-sitting.

We pushed through the door of the house and before I could even speak, my mother attacked me, swinging her fists and grabbing at my long hair. She never noticed Jill or didn't care who was standing with me. She could be volatile like this. Without warning. No matter who was around. She was raging mad because Coconut and I had cleaned out the freezer while they were off on their trip. Every day, we had steak for lunch and dinner. And we drank the supervisor's beer. What were we supposed to eat?

So much for meeting my mother.

In the car, Jill said, "Are you okay?"

I felt so embarrassed. I made excuses for her. I blamed myself.

"She really did want to meet you," I said.

On the way home from meeting my mother, I could tell something was on her mind. She kept turning and staring at me. Then she'd stare out the windshield as farm after farm waxed and waned in our side windows. She was holding my hand on the console between the seats, deep in thought. It was a clear night. Crisp and cold. Small aircraft blinked across the sky. We were listening to 38 Special. Low-lying fog sat heavy on the fields. I loped the Firebird along the county road in fourth gear, barely on the throttle. I always felt safe and calm with Jill.

She kept turning to look at me. I smiled at her each time. Then she reached and turned down the radio. "I need to tell you something. I'm leaving this spring after graduation."

"Leaving?"

"I'm going to college in Murfreesboro. I'm moving in with my sister."

I let my foot off the gas. I had no idea she was moving in with her sister, who I knew didn't approve of me.

The Basement

1981

Tuesday was my off day at the gas station, and Jill invited me to hang-out at her house. But I wasn't expecting to see cars lined up in the driveway and in front of their house. I parked on the street a couple of houses down and walked back. I had no idea they were having a party. Not at 10 a.m. on a Tuesday. Jill hadn't mentioned it.

I knocked on the door.

Jill answered with a sweet smile. "Hey. Come in." She stepped aside.

The house seemed empty, which added to the weirdness.

"Where's the party," I said.

"Party?"

"All the cars," I said, pointing toward the road.

"Oh," she said. "Every Tuesday my mother hosts a Bible study from our church."

"Are we going?"

She laughed. "No, of course not. Unless you'd like to go."

"No, I'm good. I'll pass."

She laughed again.

"What?" I said.

"You look like you've seen a ghost."

I thought for sure I'd been setup.

"Come on," she said, grabbing my hand, leading me out of the foyer.

The kitchen was off the living room and a door leading to the basement was open. I could hear singing wafting up from the Bible study. I heard a piano accompanying them.

I took a seat on the couch beside Jill and kept my eye on the basement door. What were they doing down there? I imagined them burning incense and holding crosses. I had never been around religious people who held services at their homes, and after the singing I heard them praying with ever increasing volume. I had never heard praying like that. The only prayers I ever heard were before NASCAR races. Prayers for the might of the military, for safe racing, for protection of the drivers and crew. But what was going on in the basement was all weird to me—strange medicine. I had no idea what they were doing down there. I'd never read the Bible. Sure, I'd picked up a few stories about the Bible along the way—Moses and Pharaoh, Noah and the ark. Simple stuff. I knew Jesus hung on a cross. We got Easter baskets on account of it, but I had no idea why they crucified him. I never investigated religious stuff. And I was afraid they'd get me down there and not let me out until I confessed my sins, and I wasn't into public shaming. I felt enough shame already.

Jill never pressured me, but I think deep-down she wanted me to believe in God, in the Bible, and go to church. But I didn't want anything to do with religion. Still, I didn't want to disappoint Jill.

Eventually, the Bible study ended, and the women made their way upstairs. Jill's mother introduced me to a few of them, then the house got quiet, as everyone made their way out the door.

Jill's mother stood in the living room and made small talk. I think she was trying to be nice. Maybe since she'd just finished worshipping and talking about God, she felt this was her Christian duty. I couldn't be sure if it was fake or genuine. But I could tell she was making an effort to move past the night she banned me from seeing Jill. Then she surprised me.

"You should go to church with us on Sunday, if that's okay with your parents," her mother said.

I felt my face tighten. I waited for Jill to rescue me, but she was waiting for my answer as well. "I, I think I can sometime." Trying to be sketchy but open to the idea.

Her mother said, "Be at the house at 10:00 a.m. on Sunday. You can ride with us."

With that, she turned and walked to the door leading to the basement and descended.

Jill said, "Are you coming?"

I figured it would be safer than a basement full of religious lunatics. But I feared the church wouldn't be any better.

I said, "You really want me to go?"

She perked up. "Of course I do. Spending time with you is what I want."

"Even if it means at church, where I haven't been since being a child."

"Your family doesn't attend church?"

"You're kidding, right?"

She looked at me as if she might have offended me.

I said, "I don't have a suit or nothing."

"The great thing about our church is the casual dress."

"What does that mean?"

She hesitated. "Casual dress means blue jeans and an oxford shirt."

"Gotcha," I said. But I wasn't sure what she meant by an oxford shirt. I figured Coconut might know. "Okay. This Sunday. I'll be here."

She smiled and kissed me.

The Lord's Chapel

1981

The following Sunday, Coconut helped dress me. I had on a pair of jeans and an oxford shirt—purchased from where my grandmother worked at Draper and Darwin on Main Street in Franklin.

"And don't wear that trucker's wallet," Coconut said. He'd always hated it and loved the opportunity to rip it from me. "It makes you look a wanna-be truck driver. And ditch the buck knife."

"I know better than wear a knife to church."

He raised his eyebrows and smirked.

But I had no idea what was acceptable, so I followed his directions.

I parked on the side of the road in front of Jill's house at 9:55. Two wheels in the grass, two wheels on pavement. The wooden front door was open. I could see through the storm door into the living room. I knocked. Jill came to the door. She was smiling, wearing blue jeans.

Jill opened the door, and I slid past her into the foyer.

"Sorry, I was brushing my teeth," she said.

"That's okay," I said, glad that her father hadn't come to the door. I needed Jill to be somewhat of a shield.

"You look nice," she said, grabbing my hand and leading me into the heart of the house.

The Lord's Chapel

"So do you."

"Are you nervous? Your hands are cold."

"A little," I admitted. "But I'm fine."

I wanted to say I was terrified.

"Come in and have a seat. My parents are almost ready. Sit on the couch, if you'd like. I need to grab my shoes. I'll be right back."

I sat on the tiger-striped couch. I watched *Meet the Press* on their console television near a brick fireplace.

Her mother appeared from the back and said, "How are you?"

My face flushed. I tried to speak, "I . . . I, I'm fine."

"Well, you look nice," she said.

"You do, too." *Why did I say that?* I didn't want her to take it the wrong way.

"Well, we're almost ready," she said.

Then she disappeared down the long hall and into a bedroom. I could hear her father's gruff voice at the back of the house.

Five minutes after I arrived, Jill and her parents stood before me ready for church.

"Good morning," her father said, not jovial or rude. I could tell he was working hard to be nice. Maybe some Christian duty restrained him as well, or he could've been fulfilling Jill's wishes. Maybe she'd said, "Dad, please don't be mean to him."

I said, "Nice to see you."

"Let's load up," he said.

Jill took my hand and led me out the door. We piled into the green Cadillac. Sitting inside it was surreal. I never thought I'd be riding in it on my way to church.

Her father put his arm across the back of the front-bench seat and turned his head to look through the back windshield, never once glancing at us in the backseat.

The church sat on a small hill just outside the city limits of Brentwood. The sun passed in and out of low-grazing clouds. Leaves hung heavy on the trees surrounding the parking lot. Birds were in flight, moving around from tree-to-tree, from branch-to-branch.

The name of the church sounded odd. Jill hadn't mentioned the name. So I stared at the sign at the roadway that read: *The*

Lord's Chapel. It didn't look like a traditional church with cross and steeple. It was more an octagon school-looking building. I learned later they had a thousand members and ran two services on Sunday.

We got out of the car and walked toward the entrance of the church.

Jill's father said, "Is it alligator-wrestling day or snake-handling day?"

"Stop, Sanford," her mother said. Then pushed him toward the door of the church. "Don't mind him," she said to me.

Her father laughed and smacked me on the back. "I'm just messing with you, son. It's not that bad. Come on."

I smiled as if I knew he had been joking all along. But I wanted to score brownie points with her parents, and I was almost willing to handle snakes.

Jill said, "He's just being smart-alecky."

The church had no pews, instead there were rows and rows of chairs. Sound panels hung on the walls, which puzzled me. I figured somebody needed toning down. The stage had no pulpit, instead there were four chairs against the wall at the back of the stage, beneath a pool of water built into the wall and on the wall above it hung a large wooden cross. Three men in suits occupied the chairs on the stage. A band with a drummer, two guitar players, and a horn section sat on one end of the massive stage, a baby grand piano sat on the floor beside the band.

Jill's mother led us to a row of chairs, and we had a seat. Jill positioned herself next to me with her parents on the other side of her, creating a barrier that helped my nerves. But I felt a drop of sweat roll from under my arm and down my side, like a drop of blood. I looked over at Jill.

"Sorry my father did that," she said. "Sometimes he thinks he's being funny. It's his way of breaking the ice. They are both happy that you are here."

"I hope so," I said.

Her comments reminded me of why I was there. I needed to hear this, but I didn't dare look their way. I only wanted this to be over. It felt like the doctor's office, but with more people. A lot more people.

An older man with a cross necklace had a few announcements about Bible studies, missionaries, and ways you could connect with other Christians in small groups throughout the city. Then the music started, and I understood the need for sound panels. An energetic clean-cut man led the music, and it was lively. People clapped and swayed. Some raised their hands with upturned palms in complete submission, as if God himself might reach down and take them. Their very breath seemed to create the presence of God in that place. No hymnals, no words on a screen. I'd never seen or heard anything like this. The lyrics weren't anything like Bob Seger, and I had never clapped in public. Maybe as an ovation or something, but never to music. And they sang about Jesus for an hour before they got around to telling you about Jesus for another hour.

And Jill's mother had a lovely voice. Her father's, not so lovely. Jill wasn't singing. I'm not sure if she did this so I wouldn't feel left out, but it helped. Still, I stood beside them—woodened and lost. Looking for the exits.

A woman on the other side of me was reading my mind. My mind felt exposed to her somehow. I'm not sure why I suddenly feared her or why I felt she had access to my mind. Probably the residual of an acid trip only a month before. In certain stressful situations I found myself hallucinating again, and this woman was freaking me out. I felt I might come undone. I felt dirty. Unclean. I stared at the floor. She wore black dress pants. Thick ankles in a pair of pumps.

By the end of the songs, some were crying. Some had danced themselves into a sweat. Some stood the way Jill and I did. Just there. Occupying space. It was all so weird. Every few minutes Jill would look at me and smile. She'd squeeze my hand. She had no idea all of this was going on inside my mind. I could put on a good front. I knew how to keep the battle hidden. And even though it seemed so weird, I felt something real.

After the singing, a small man in cowboy boots and what looked like a hand-me-down western suit stood to preach. He had a way with the congregation. I could tell they adored him, and it calmed me. He wasn't a fire and brimstone preacher or dry-as-toast like the ones conducting funerals. He tried to make them laugh and did. I didn't catch the humor in it. But nothing about him was phony. Still, his forty-five-minute sermon was long. And I was sure I never wanted to come back.

In the parking lot, on the way back to the Cadillac, Jill didn't ask me if I liked the service. But I'm sure she was wondering how I felt about her holy-roller, charismatic church. I'm not sure what I thought about it. Mostly, I was scared and tired. It was a fight to the end with the woman trying to steal my innermost thoughts.

Back at Jill's house, her mother said, "Would you like to stay for lunch?"

Everything inside me wanted to take a ride and smoke a joint to clear my head, to get back inside the Firebird again. I was nervous around her mother, as if I'd been raised in a barn and was now being invited into a house of sophistication where I knew none of the rules. But I saw the hopeful look Jill gave me when her mother asked, so I said, "Sure."

Hefty

2019

Hefty is unlike the other cows on the farm. She's not scrappy like Brown Sugar. She's very laidback and sweet and patient. Doesn't get in a hurry or take flight easily. She's smooth and steady in her gait. She has short legs and what we call a "sagging chin" with the body of a bull. She looks like her father, Big Bull, who we sold a year ago. Big Bull would always make a groaning sound when we fed him pellets. Much like we do when handed our favorite desert. And Hefty makes the same noise, so we love to single her out and stuff her with pellets, because we miss Big Bull. She stands at the fence near the end of our driveway. She watches for us to come outside in the yard, then she gets our attention. And for this we love her and for this we reward her.

A few months ago, back when Cowboy Tommy came to work our cows—which means he dewormed them, put in fly tags, and checked them for pregnancy—he said there was no need in checking Hefty. She looked due any day, and it would be her first baby. But three months passed with no baby, and for three months we checked on her daily.

Jill does the morning rounds. She walks among them with a checklist that has the number of each cow and how many calves we have on the farm. We lost a red bull calf once. We have no idea how he came up missing. We looked and searched. Nothing. So, every day Jill counts and checks on their welfare.

Each day, I'd ask about Hefty, and for three months she'd said, "Not yet."

At that time, every cow on the farm, except for Hefty and #3, had had a baby. And while we were in Mississippi visiting my daughter, my father sent me a Facebook message telling me Hefty had finally had her baby.

When I got home, I found Hefty's baby in the woods at the edge of the pasture. Hefty had stashed her in the shade while she grazed 10-yards away. The sweltering sun beat down on their backs as they grazed. It was the hottest June on record. Pushing 95 degrees with a heat index of 104. Too hot to be having babies.

I approached the calf and Hefty came trotting across the pasture like, "Don't go waking up my baby. I just got her down for a nap." And I'd never seen Hefty trot for anything. Usually she plodded along like she had weights on her legs. Seeing her trot made me laugh. And her baby was a beauty. Black as coal. And she licked his furry back and nudged it up and away from me. She was proud of her baby.

Hefty's baby meant that #3 was the last cow that hadn't calved, and I went to check on her across the pasture where she was grazing. And I noticed a string of red substance and a huge red bubble hanging from her rear. It frightened and sickened me.

I took a picture and sent it to my father and stepmother. My stepmother said it meant she would be having the calf soon. Maybe within the hour. And I've never seen a cow give birth and wanted to video it and maybe put it on Facebook. I had two good hours of light left in the day, so I rushed home and got my Go-Pro.

A light rain fell and cooled the sultry afternoon, and I followed #3 around as she grazed with the birth matter hanging from her rear.

And I watched.

I waited.

Hefty

I followed her over hills and through ditches for two hours with no birth, as she looked back at me every now and then, as if to say, "I don't want to be on Facebook. Leave me alone."

As the evening dissolved into the mist above the hills, I stood in silvery light on a hillside with #3, #26, #18, and with Hefty and her new baby boy. Green rolling hills before us. Wet grass stretching toward a wooded area. And we were all just existing there. Some chewed their cuds. Some grazed. The calves looked at me like, "What are you doing out here at night?"

Hefty lay in the wet grass with her baby boy by her side, watching me. And I have to say, everything was all right in that moment, the world wasn't a cruel place. Not then. Not there. Not on that smoky hillside. And I figured a little speech might be appropriate. Maybe a confession, because they were allowing me this moment of serenity in the secret lives of cows. I told them, "I know the farm takes your babies, but you get to be a herd on this farm. You're not confined to some dusty lot and treated like you really are a number. And I know that doesn't lessen the pain. And Hefty, I know that baby you cherish tonight will one day be taken. That's the nature of the business. And it's not that much different with farmers. Loved ones are taken, and we are not sure where they go either. And we bawl and scream. And I could tell you about where your babies end up, but that's information that won't do you any good tonight. So, let's just enjoy this moment we have together on this hillside, in the misty late afternoon. The alternative is to dread the future."

I thought of Bob Seger's song, "We've Got Tonite." (I always think of Seger songs.)

And I told them about that song.

I said, "I could sing it for you, but you wouldn't feel it in your bones the way I felt it the first time I heard it, because I grew up letting Bob Seger tell me how to feel. The longing in his voice filled many nights like this. But I won't sing. I'm going home to give #3 room to have her baby without having to worry about it ending up on Facebook." I looked to where #3 stood and said, "You're welcome."

Before I turned to leave, I stood there a little longer with bullfrog croaks rising to a crescendo in a nearby pond, while lightning bugs flashed their bulbs in the arena of nature. And in that moment, I did not know I would be burying Hefty's baby the following day in our cow cemetery. I found her baby boy on a hillside with Hefty standing over him. I could not resuscitate him. I tried. I poured a bucket of water on him. Slapped his body. "Please wake-up," I cried. "Please!"

I wasn't sure how long he'd been dead. Wasn't sure what had happened to him. The heat index hit 105 that day, so maybe something heat related. I'm not sure. But I screamed profanity at the sky. The cows stopped grazing and looked at Hefty. They looked at me standing over the dead calf. Brown Sugar approached and bumped noses with Hefty, as if to say, "I lost a baby, too."

I wondered if they were aware of what was happening.

I even prayed for God to resurrect the dead calf.

I know. Crazy, right?

But nothing.

Hefty's first baby boy was gone and #3's baby stood beside her. Born in the night sometime after I left them in the dark field. One taken from the field, the other left behind.

What Anne Lamott said, *But the bad news is that whatever you use to keep the pain at bay robs you of flecks and nuggets of gold that feeling grief will give you.*

The Dumpster Man

2015

At the psych hospital, I was the writing teacher for the adolescents in the morning, and the teacher for the children in the afternoon. Basically, I just handed them busy work or helped them complete assignments sent from their schools. Sometimes autistic children were admitted so the psychiatrists could adjust their meds and monitor these changes. Once we had an autistic child who loved sounds, especially ticks, so to calm him I'd given him a cooking timer that I used in my writing class with the adolescents. He would sit at a desk in the classroom and listen continuously, as if hidden messages were being tapped out in a code only he could understand. It kept him occupied. Without it, he would kick and claw and scream. He'd driven us all crazy. Then he heard the dumpster man.

One day he heard the dumpster truck in the parking lot—raising the dumpster above its bed and banging the dumpster clean. Unable to see it, he began quizzing us about the sound. Maybe it was the loud banging combined with the beeping of the warning signal. I'm not sure. But he asked question after question.

"What is it?"

"Why does it make that noise?"

"What's a dumpster?"

"Why do you put trash in it?"

"Where does he take the trash?"

We explained the process. He wanted to know how it lifted it. One of the psych techs told him it worked like this. He put his arms out and said, "It hugs it and lifts it up. Then dumps it and puts it back down."

This fascinated him, and he begged to see the dumpster man doing his dumpster job. He wanted to watch and hear, so staff started watching for the dumpster truck. But two weeks went by and no one could catch him. Then one day I saw him turning into the parking lot. I jumped on the phone, called the children's unit, and told the psych tech that the dumpster man was in the parking lot and to hurry and bring the boy.

By the time I got to the parking lot, he had finished emptying the dumpster and was headed toward the main highway. But I could see the tip of his elbow extruding through the window, so I yelled as loud as I could, hoping he would hear, also realizing hospital administration might hear as well.

Just when I thought we'd lost our opportunity the dumpster man stopped and turned to look at me with his head extruding from the window where his elbow had been.

I ran to him and said, "There's a little boy here that's in love with you." I realized how weird it sounded after I'd said it.

But the dumpster man laughed and said, "Everybody loves me."

I said, "I mean, he loves what you do. He's fascinated by the way you empty the dumpster, so would you mind doing it again so he can watch you?"

"Sure," he said all syrupy-sweet with a Jack-o-lantern face.

I said, "Great! I'll get him."

When I turned from the dumpster man, the psych tech had the boy already standing behind me.

I bent down and told the boy, "He's going to do it again so you can watch."

The dumpster man had jumped from his truck and had joined us. He said, "I can do better than that. What you say I let you in the passenger seat, then you can get a real good look."

The Dumpster Man

I was caught off guard. It could get me fired if I went through with it. Had administration heard me yelling for the dumpster man? Were they looking out their windows, watching us? I had a decision to make. I looked down at the boy and said, "Do you want to ride in the truck and watch him empty the dumpster?"

The little boy nodded.

The dumpster man said, "Come on around here, partner. Let me move my cooler out of the seat and you can jump right in."

He removed his cooler and I figured it would be better if I jumped in there with him, so I grabbed him under the arms and hoisted him up, then I climbed inside.

I wondered if my supervisor was watching from his office window, afraid he would be standing in the parking lot when the ride was over.

The dumpster man shut our door and crossed the front of the truck and climbed behind the wheel.

"Here we go," the dumpster man said. He released the airbrakes and the truck exhaled and lunged slightly on its haunches. Then we moved toward the dumpster, and when the arms of the dumpster truck picked up the dumpster, the boy said, "I love the way it hugs it."

What made this boy—who feared hugging, being a trait of autism—feel thrilled about the way the dumpster truck hugged the dumpster?

Then the dumpster went up and over the truck as it jumped up and down on its shock absorbers. *Boom, boom, boom*, as the man worked his levers.

The boy smiled. I'd never seen him smile. And if I could have frozen that moment in his life, I would have. But the world doesn't work that way. Not for him. Not for you and me. It was over, and the man said, "How'd you like that partner?"

That afternoon the boy sat calmly in front of the cooking timer, a little more aware of the dumpster man's work. He knew how it hugged the dumpster. He could picture its movement. The secret man behind the noises revealed. When someone asked him about the experience, he said, "I love the way it hugs it."

Gone in 60 Seconds

1981

Hearing them speak in tongues at the Lord's Chapel was like listening to a cooking timer for Morse code. The first time I heard someone babble—for I do not know any other way of describing it—I thought it weird and disruptive. Like someone had sucked the joy I found in worship from the room. It came on sudden. Someone spoke in tongues and someone else in another location in the chapel called out what was supposed to be an interpretation, "Thus sayeth the Lord..." Then from there it always seemed to be a warning about sin and corruption in the world. Like the beeping of the Dumpster Man's truck.

One Sunday, it got weirder when an evangelist appeared.

That morning, Jill's mother had mentioned a guest evangelist. "Today, Evangelist John Wesley Fletcher will be speaking."

I thought of Evangelist Ernest Angley on television. I always laughed when Ernest whispered "ba-bee" in deaf ears, trying to get them to repeat the word. He even smacked their foreheads, pushing them ever so slightly into the waiting arms of ushers. And when he got happy, he had this one-step-jig we used to imitate while playing sports in the neighborhood. Whenever we hit a basket in basketball or scored a touchdown, we'd do the *Ernest Angley*. We'd hop on one foot and say, "Ba-bee."

But this evangelist didn't have the same feel. He seemed more like a psychic, than a healer. He told one man, "The doctors gave you no hope, but God says . . ."

The man said, "How did you know that?"

We had entered the twilight zone.

I ducked down afraid he'd expose me as the fraud I was in that place. Only there to get a girl and please her family. That fraud.

He asked Jill's father to stand. Her father swallowed hard and stood.

The evangelist said, "You will be signing some important documents in the near future."

Then he went on to tell him what he should do. Sure enough, a week later his mother died, and since he was an only child, he inherited the farm in North Carolina.

He eyed me when he finished with Jill's father, then padded up the aisle looking for new prey.

Sure, he smacked foreheads like Ernest Angley and the ushers caught his prey when they fell backwards. Some stayed down and out for ten minutes or longer. They were placed on their backs in the aisles with arms by their sides like cadavers in a morgue.

The evangelist said, "Don't you worry about them. They will be fine. God has taken them offline to deal with a few things."

I wondered how that worked. I was suspicious, but something felt real, which scared me. And like the autistic boy hearing the Dumpster Man for the first time, I knew something was out there, beyond me, and I wouldn't need blotter acid to find it. Still, I could not comprehend it. And my heart raced.

The evangelist said, "Someone has a thumping heart. I hear it."

My head shot up. I looked over at Jill beside me, wondering if she could hear the beating of my heart. She gave me a puzzled look.

"It's about to beat out of your chest. You need to get up and come down here to the altar and give your beating heart to Christ," the evangelist said. Then quieter he said, "Hurry. We're waiting."

I looked over at Jill again. She smiled, so I figured I was just being paranoid, but my heart was pounding. Really pounding.

The evangelist said, "There are eighteen people here that will never see the face of the Lord unless you leave your seat and come down to the altar. I'll give you sixty seconds."

The chapel tilted slightly on its axis, trying to shake me free from the chair. The background noise of a piano accompanied the evangelist's countdown. "One, two, three . . ."

Like Poe's heart beneath the floorboards, my heart kept pounding. I was sure the whole congregation could hear it.

"You have ten seconds." Then the evangelist purred, "Jesus is waiting."

I left my seat and pushed by Jill's parents seated on the end of the row. I went down to the altar and wanted to shriek, "I am the one with the beating heart! Me! This heart! It beats! Oh, God it beats!" But my words strangled in my throat. I wanted to cry out, but only bawled. I had no voluntary choice. I stood at the altar. Plucked from the fire. He cracked my chest open and held my heart before the people. He palmed it—turning it over as if he'd caught a fish and wanted to see the colors of the body and watch the movement of the gills. Then he prayed for the prey he'd trapped at the altar.

We didn't know then that Evangelist John Wesley Fletcher was the one who'd introduced Jim Baker to Jessica Hahn, the woman Baker and Fletcher sexually assaulted and paid hush money. Their dirty deeds in the Florida hotel room were still hidden. Fletcher allegedly died of AIDS at the age of 56. But it's not about what the two of them did together. It's about what they did to that woman in the hotel room. It's about the way he gave everyone from Brentwood to Kalamazoo the same 60 seconds to see the face of the Lord or be damned forever.

Soon, the nation watched Jim Baker ball up in a fetus position in the backseat of his lawyer's car, weeping crocodile tears beneath those huge glasses. All of this would happen much later. But that Sunday I was hoodwinked into believing I was one of the eighteen people who would never see the face of the Lord unless I went down to the altar. I just didn't know—had never even imagined in a thousand ages—that I'd be the victim of eternal manipulation. I had vowed to never be tricked again after my mother left us. I'd vowed to stay alert, but here I was bawling for the first time since that night. In public.

Either I went down to the altar or I died in that chair. I can tell you I had no choice. I'd almost OD on PCP once. I knew the margins, the edges, the boundaries, the outskirts of hell. Then the drug ran its course and life retrieved me. But with God, you get a whole new beginning. You become a new creation, but not really. Not here. Not in this place.

I'm sure there were more than eighteen people at the altar that day. Someone was a farce, someone didn't belong. A dude actually elbowed me out of the way to stand in front of me. But it wasn't about what he did, it was about standing there before a thousand people and not knowing I was standing before a thousand people. It was about admitting something was wrong with me, instead of hiding from public shame. And if I had been the nineteenth person to go down to the altar, I would have still had the same experience. Numbers had nothing to do with it. It would just mean the evangelist heard God wrong. He wasn't infallible, so it turned out.

After the evangelist prayed, I went back to my seat. Jill's parents reached out. They smiled. They had prayed for this moment. Probably believing it would never happen. I kept bawling. Living water flowed from my eyes, and they kept hugging me. And I loved the way they hugged me, and if you ask me today why I'm a Christian, it would have much to do with the way Jill and her parents welcomed me into their family that day and God into his. And I can't tell you how to find God, because the Holy Spirit can't be charted or controlled. Who understands how God woos us? But He wooed me. And that must count for something.

What Thomas Merton said: *Father, I love You Whom I do not know, and I embrace You Whom I do not see, and I abandon myself to You Whom I have offended, because You love in me Your only begotten Son. You see Him in me, You embrace Him in me, because He has willed to identify Himself completely with me by that love which brought Him to death, for me, on the Cross.*[29]

Brand New

1981

Outwardly I was the same, but inwardly I was being renewed with each passing day. I even got baptized to prove this inward work was at play. Pastor Bruce Coble baptized me at the Lord's Chapel. He stood beside me in his rubber overalls. Those big hands of his pushing me down as the water gave way and rushed around my head. Then he pulled me out. Water dripped from my mullet and big nose. Everyone clapped. I smiled. Bruce gave me a wide grin. Jill's parents gave me a cross necklace after the service. Everything was so brand-new and hopeful. I was clean. Sins washed away. I was sure I'd never sin again. I vowed to go back to the streets of Franklin and win my old friends to the Lord. But I knew nothing about the Bible or how to tell anyone how I changed. I only knew I was in love with the Lord. He had changed me. I never doubted the wave of love that filled my soul at the Lord's Chapel, even years later when I learned the truth about John Wesley Fletcher. After being baptized, I tried reading the Bible, but I couldn't understand it.

One night on a date with Jill, I asked her, "How do you read the Bible? Where should I start?"

She said, "Let's go ask my mother. She will know."

We drove to her house and found her mother sitting in the living room reading a book. Her eyes widened when she saw us.

Jill said, "Robbie wants to know where he should read in the Bible."

Her face relaxed. She said, "Well, read the Book of John."

"Okay," I said.

She said, "Do you have a Bible?"

"No, ma'am," I said.

She found me a Bible and handed it to me, not realizing how confused I would be later when I discovered four books about John—The Book of John and 1, 2, 3 John. This confused me. I didn't know which one she meant for me to read. So, I read 1 John. "If we claim to be without sin, we deceive ourselves and the truth is not in us" (1 John 1:8). That floored me. Up to this point, I thought you had to be somewhat perfect and without sin. I read nothing but 1 John for a while. I'd slowly read it, then reread it. I was having trouble understanding the concepts and lessons, and the next time I visited Jill's house, her mother asked me if I was reading the Bible. I told her about the four books of John, and I think she realized my learning disabilities, and she said, "Why don't you start meeting with me once a week, and we will talk about God and the Bible or whatever."

Wanting to be in her good graces, I agreed. And this started a discussion that led to me telling her my life story. She never asked, "What's the matter with you?" She never had an agenda of *fixing me*, it seemed. She seemingly asked, "What matters most to you?" It was the key to my healing. I felt safe. I trusted her. Someone believed in me, someone was listening. And she wanted to know about my family and why my parents divorced. I told her the story of my mother and the supervisor, about seeing them through Carl's windshield. And from this point forward, she started calling me her son. Every time she introduced me to her friends, she would say, "Have you met my son, Robbie?"

Now I had a real mother-figure, and I'd also found a family—something I'd always wanted. Jill's mother forgave me for almost killing her daughter and accepted and loved me in such a safe way that I started to understand God's grace. She took a risk on me and allowed me to become a better person. Then it all changed again. I let her down.

Fifty Dollar Man

1981

I broke open the packaging as Jill watched. Then we hid it beneath the bathroom sink—back behind the bowl cleaner and extra toilet tissue—and the waiting began. We kissed, and she drove off in her mother's Cadillac. She said she'd call me when she arrived home.

I paced a while. Ate some potato chips. Drank a Coke. I could not stay in the house. I was afraid I would look too soon, and it would give a false reading. So I went out to the garage and sat in the Firebird. I turned the ignition and pushed AC/DC into the tape deck, then remembered I was trying to change my listening habits. I'd discovered Christian rock but had to force myself to listen to it. I was trying to have the clean heart I'd received a few months before at the Lord's Chapel. But some force inside me still hadn't been reckoned with.

I sat there watching the clock, as chemicals arranged our fate. Three Christian rock songs killed the time. Back inside, I went to the bathroom. Stalled a second. Prayed. Looked at myself in the mirror. I thought, *Are you ready for this? Do you really want to know?* I wanted to be with her forever, but what do you know when you're eighteen? You don't even know yourself, especially when you've been on drugs. Some say the moment you take drugs is the moment when you stop developing emotionally. If that's true, I was emotionally fourteen back then. Now there was the possibility of a baby.

I retrieved the pregnancy test from under the sink. The plus sign was there. I looked away. Then looked back to make sure my eyes weren't playing tricks on me. And I waited for Jill to call. When I told her, she cried. She said her parents were going to kill her. I told her we'd get married. Things would work out. Love conquers all, right?

We sat on her parent's tiger-striped couch. In the evening time. Jill's mother sat in one chair, her father in another one. Jill and I sat on the couch holding hands. Just the four of us. Her mother's cancer was back, but she hadn't told the family yet, but Jill and I had something to tell the family.

Her mother with folded arms and rigid body let our confession hang in the air without a response. Her father steaming mad took over and said, "I'll give you fifty dollars, and you can hit the road." Sure, it was 1981, but, still, fifty dollars wouldn't get me far—not as far as he wanted to send me.

Jill's mother said, "Now, Sanford, you know that's not the answer." She unfolded her arms but kept the bewildered where-did-we-go-wrong-look on her face. She exuded acceptance while accentuating adversity. She continued, pausing between carefully chosen words. Maybe even rehearsed words. "You and Jill have made a mistake. You've complicated things. But let's try to move forward. Are you planning to get married? But don't think you have to get married. Robbie, we can help Jill raise this baby. Marry her because you love her. Take your time. Think about all of this. There's no need to rush into wedding plans. Shame should not be the motivating factor here."

Jill said, "We've talked about it. We love each other. I know he's the right one for me. I love him, obviously. So, we'll make it. We can overcome this. It's not how I envisioned my life."

Her mother said, "Robbie, how do you feel?"

"I feel the same way. I love Jill. I'm sorry you are going through this."

We established a wedding date. Valentine's Day, a Sunday afternoon in 1982.

What Frederick Buechner said: *Even the saddest things can become, once we have made peace with them, a source of wisdom and strength for the journey that still lies ahead.*

Father and Son

2019

I lifted Hefty's dead calf from the ground and put him in the back of the utility vehicle. I drove toward the barn. At the bottom of the hill, I looked back to where the cows dotted the field with their babies to make sure Hefty wasn't following. She was grazing, so I stopped at the barn and got a shovel. An early full moon was luminous over the barn. The sky had reddened in the west. I put the shovel in the back with the calf, then looked across the road to my father's house. I'd called him thirty minutes before to tell him about the dead calf, expecting some urgency. But he was in no hurry. Probably eating supper.

I drove along the base of the hill and past the pond in the bottom. The Buffalo River takes a hard-right turn just beyond the pond and flows parallel with Highway 13. Branches scraped over the cab of the utility vehicle as I approached the cemetery that's near a ravine. Overarching trees make the cemetery a cool spot on the farm. I cut the motor and got out. A gentle breeze pulsated through the trees like waves of intercessory prayer, as bullfrogs sang a doxology at the edge of the pond—deep and resonate. Mama Moo was the last cow buried at the cemetery. We buried her after she developed cancer-eye. A gruesome disease that attracted a congregation of flies. Nothing could be done. She was at peace now.

What Larry Brown said: *The lives of cows are fickle and uncertain. One day they may look fine and the next day be dead as a hammer.*[30]

I could hear an occasional car on Highway 13, as I took the shovel and began digging next to Mama Moo, wiping sweat from my forehead, wondering when my father would arrive. I figured he wasn't coming.

Thirty minutes later, I heard the tractor start at the barn. The engine revved and the sound of the motor crept closer. When he rounded the corner at the edge of the pond, I leaned on my shovel and watched him get out of the tractor. He walked to where I stood at the open grave, side-stepping manure on his way. He had on a pair of black shorts, black tennis shoes with black socks pulled up over his calves. He peered at the calf and said, "Well, what do you know, a little bull calf."

I wondered if he'd even seen Hefty's calf. He was supposed to be watching Hefty and checking on the calf. He was on duty that day. He watches the cows on the weekend. It was late Saturday afternoon. I had checked on them because I wondered if #3 had had her baby. This was when I found Hefty's dead calf. And anger rose up in me. It always emerges when I feel he is neglecting farm work. He'd bought an old muscle car and had started restoring it. At times, I feel like he neglects farm work because he's piddling with the car.

He watched me dig, then offered, "Things like this happen on the farm. Sometimes you never know what causes them to die."

I clenched my jaw and said, "You and I played a part in this."

He opened his mouth to say something but didn't.

I kept digging.

I knew he would have been unable to save the calf—only find it dead as I had. Something had happened internally. Who knows what? My father was right. You never know what happens sometimes. Farms have mysterious deaths. I was just mad and took it out on him. I held him responsible for my disappointment.

Eventually, he grabbed the shovel and helped dig. But he's been short of breath lately and stopped after four or five turns of the spade.

I realized we had switched places. The father becoming the son, the son becoming the father. But what does becoming the father mean? I've always identified with being the rebellious son. Now I'm the one that must forgive.

Forgive my father for wanting to restore a car and discover joy and freedom in his old age.

Forgive my father for taking me on that car ride with Carl to see my mother at the supervisor's house.

Forgive my mother for leaving without saying a word.

Forgive myself for being a wayward son.

You and I always play a part in forgiveness.

What Gerald G. Jampolsky said: *Inner peace is experienced as we learn to forgive the world and everyone in it, and thereby see everyone, including ourselves, as blameless.*[31]

And we must ask ourselves the hard questions:

"What's really going on inside of me?"

"Why am I angry?"

"Why am I holding this person captive?"

I demand my parents give me a constant and ongoing apology. I demand it always be present in their actions. I demand it with my anger when I can't openly say it.

I demand imprisonment.

But I must liberate.

I must be compassionate as my Heavenly Father is compassionate.

What Richard Rohr said: *It has become acceptable for some time in America to remain 'wound identified' (that is using one's victimhood as one's identity, one's ticket to sympathy, and one's excuse for not serving), instead of using the wound to 'redeem the world,' as we see in Jesus and many people who turn their wounds into sacred wounds that liberate both themselves and others.*[32]

I finished covering the calf with dirt, then I hoped for a resurrection in some field in heaven.
    Do all cows go to heaven?
    Are they freed of methane gas?
    Are they forgiven for their involvement in climate change?
    What say so do they have in it?

Valentine's Day

1982

Friends and family walked into the Lord's Chapel in Brentwood, Tennessee, on Valentine's day. They found their seats. They whispered to one another. Some bowed their heads in prayer, knowing God was our only chance at a happy life ever after. Because even though we'd turned the corner in our relationship with God, the odds were against us. Teenage marriages are two to three times more likely to end in divorce.

The music started promptly at two o'clock then Jill's father led her down the aisle to where I stood at the altar with her brother as my best man. Her mother sat on the front row weak with cancer that would eventually end her life. Silent cells multiplying with each crescendo of the wedding march.

Jill and I stood before two hundred people that Valentine's Day. We also knelt at an altar belonging to the local rental store, while a woman sang, "Bind Us Together, Lord." We looked over at one another with smiles. What kind of crazy God would bring about the possibility of such a union, in such disarray?

What Charles Haddon Spurgeon said: *Since his only and sole object is your good, incline your ear and come to him. Hearken diligently, and let the good word sink into your soul. It may be that the hour is come in which you shall enter upon that new life which is the beginning of heaven.*[33]

Tuesday Bible Study

1982

Jill's mother loved her Tuesday Bible study. When her cancer returned, she didn't shut it down or ask them to find a new location. Too weak to attend, she remained in her bed, and the women who attended would visit her room. Some prayed with volume, and you'd think the whole roof might lift from the house. They boldly spoke to the devil, demanding the cancer leave her body. Some spoke in low tones, confident that God had already healed her, expecting the manifestation of it later. They prayed, "We thank you for what you are going to do."

Jill's mother kept a spiral notebook on her nightstand, recording her medicine regime, writing down the day of the week and the time of day she swallowed each pill.

Jill had graduated from barber college and had taken a job in Franklin cutting hair. Her clientele was small in the beginning. We didn't make enough money to rent an apartment, so we moved into the basement and shared space with the Bible study. One more drain upon a suffering mother.

Her father took me to the top of the stairs leading down to the basement and said, "I'm head of the house and you will be head of the basement."

I wasn't sure what it meant. I'd never heard the phrase. I figured he meant I should stay in the basement and not come

Tuesday Bible Study

upstairs, so I said, "Okay." I didn't care. I had everything I ever wanted, even if that meant being the *head of the basement*, because we had a baby on the way, and we were in love. We were now nineteen and free. Lovers on the bottom floor taking one last run at pre-adulthood. Things would change. We knew this.

We discovered *head of the house* controlled the thermostat upstairs, which regulated the whole house, and the *head of the house* was a descendent of Scrooge who rarely used his central heat and air system. He bragged about it being twenty-five years old and yet cold as the day he moved in.

Every night after the local news, as we lay cool as cucumbers, we'd hear the boards above our heads creak under his weight, and he'd ram the thermostat above 90 degrees. Then the dinosaur out back would puff one last breath of cool air, we'd look at each other, roll our eyes into the next state, and kiss the fresh air good-bye. Then night sweats ensued.

But what can you do? Take control of your destiny?

You bet. So one night we slipped upstairs and took control of the dinosaur. We woke it up and made it bellow all night, and did so for a whole month. When the electric bill arrived in the mailbox, her father gave us an old-fashioned lecture about growing up with no A/C and sent us back to the basement to lick the sweat from our upper lips. We paid extra that month.

On Saturdays, her father would invite us up for breakfast. He'd get his griddle out from under the cabinet, plug it in and grease it up with butter. Then he'd make pancakes while telling stories of the way it used to be around there, back before I was even thought of, back before he realized a son-in-law would be living in the basement. He'd flip pancakes while sausage sizzled, and he'd tell about the time when Jill's grandmother, Mrs. Moore, lived with them after her husband died. She didn't like being left alone. It scared her. So Jill's father, wanting to make a lasting impression on how great a son-in-law he was, displayed a pistol that would keep her safe if she were there by herself. It was supposed to be a quick lesson in proper gun handling and safety, and when Ms. Moore asked him if it was loaded, he said, "I've got the safety switch on.

Watch." He pulled the trigger and a bullet shot past Mrs. Moore, into the cabinet, exiting the countertop, went through a cake on the counter, and then lodged itself in the wall.

"It's right here," he said, pointing to a section of the wall above the counter. "We covered the hole with wallpaper, but it's right here."

I laughed.

He shot back a sly grin.

Then I offered, "I bet it scared her to death."

Another sly grin. Then, "Yeah, she never wanted to see that pistol again."

There were other zany stories, and the more stories he told, the more he opened his life to me, which made me look forward to those moments on Saturday mornings when *head of the house* included the *head of the basement* in the telling and retelling of stories that made up his life. And when Jill's father came to live with us before his death, I took him to his bedroom and said, "I'm the *head of the house*, and you will be *head of the bedroom*."

Frederick Buechner said: *You fashion your story as you fashion your faith, out of the great hodgepodge of your life—the things that have happened to you and the things you've dreamed of happening. They're the raw material of both.*[34]

The Drug Dealer and the Gun

1982

Jill was bedridden the last three months of her pregnancy. And her mother was no longer in remission. Both bedridden and suffering, her father hired a housekeeper/caretaker who ended up stealing some antique jewelry. Nothing seemed to be going right. Even Jill's younger brother, who went on to play football at Alabama, was having teenage rebellion problems. The house was a hotbed of illness and nerves. And quickly becoming one of exhaustion. But I never felt one bit of animosity from Jill's parents. Mrs. Whitehurst never blamed God or quit believing that God was going to somehow redeem things. She refused to allow bitterness to accompany her cancer. She even cut a picture out of the newspaper of a starving child in Africa and pinned it to the wall beside her bed as a reminder of greater suffering in the world.

By this time, I had a job at a place that manufactured transmissions for Corvettes in an area between Brentwood and Franklin called Cool Springs. The job had great insurance, but low pay. Still, it was a move up. But I was working long hours and wasn't much help around the house. Even though I was only nineteen, I thought I could handle being a father. But providing for a baby proved to be another matter. I knew the Firebird would have to go, so I sold it and bought a Nissan Sentra. A family car. As I watched the new owner drive the Firebird out of the neighborhood, my childhood ended. Sure, I still mourn that car at times the way I do Coconut's presence in my life. Coconut and I split company after a drug dealer shoved a gun in his face. Coconut pressed charges, and I was summonsed to testify. Not sure why. I wasn't even with Coconut when it went down. I'd dropped him off in Franklin and had headed home to crash, so my testimony was irrelevant. But I was supposed to be a character witness because the defense attorney painted us as drug addicts that might just make up a tale of being robbed. And I wasn't a good witness. I wasn't a faithful friend. After becoming a Christian, I was attempting honesty in all relationships. But I had no idea of truth's consequences, so I told the truth in court with tears in my eyes again. Whatever happened in church that Sunday had opened the floodgates of emotion. I bawled like a forlorn calf whenever I opened my mouth in a public setting.

Maybe I should have painted us as choir boys in that courtroom. For what is honesty if it cost you a friendship? And this broke-off our relationship. We went separate ways. The public trial had spooked me. I wanted to distance myself from any involvement with drugs. But maybe all the public emotional outbursts proved I was coming apart at the seams. Faith in God makes you weird before it ever makes you loveable. You despise your old lifestyle, which means you will despise old friends, which means in ways that you are despising yourself. Salvation comes off as if you think you're better than them. And they're looking at you like, "Didn't I just smoke weed with him last week? Didn't he buy acid from me last month? Who is this person?" And you don't know yourself. Just as a baby doesn't know the smell is his own soiled diaper. My old friends didn't understand my tender heart. They had no idea a heart of stone had been replaced with a heart of flesh (Ezekiel 36:26). They knew nothing of such a transplant. They didn't know my bawling was the crack where the darkness leaked out.

A heart of flesh feels different from a heart of stone, and you are different. You're brand new with the same exterior. You remain stranded in skin and bones with the same corrupted mind that is being renewed. A mind that still thinks bad thoughts. A body that wants dope. And I wish I could say I quit drugs after receiving Christ in my life, but I didn't. This was why I sat in the courtroom that day trying to defend Coconut, but insisting I was a changed man, while voices in my head were telling me that nothing had really happened that Sunday I trembled beneath the evangelist's hands.

Becoming a Christian doesn't make you a new creation, not really. Yes, you are a child of God, and nothing can take that from you, but total restoration never occurs here. It's reserved for heaven. This never gets told to new converts in a way that instructs them. There's so much guilt in the beginning. Churches demand pure religion when all we are capable of is bawling, so let us bawl first and obey second. For wherever you discover bawling, it's the beginning of a healing process.

What I needed in those early years of my faith was a home, a family, a church, and a place to belong. Not a place to be pressured into being fake. God didn't need my testimony. It was too early for this. We must abide. We must learn how to become loveable, not zealous.

Even though I led a blemished life, I remained committed to the process of change. And on September 10, 1982, God gave us a baby girl, and we named her Blair.

What Jesus said: *I am the vine; you are the branches. If you remain in me and I in you, you will bear much fruit; apart from me you can do nothing.*

Reba's Trees

1982

Reba attended the Tuesday Bible study. She was a bit eccentric and believed she could heal Mrs. Whitehurst with natural herbs. She would come to the Bible study and cook godawful-smelling lunches for her, and even built flower boxes outside Mrs. Whitehurst's bedroom window so the view wouldn't be desolate. I loved this about Mrs. Whitehurst. She didn't mind surrounding herself with losers, the lost, the damned. She didn't care how they reflected on her character. She was compassionate as her heavenly father was compassionate.

One summer at the beach, a school of jellyfish stung Reba. She said it made her life go downhill. She wrote bad checks and pledged a million dollars to Jim Baker's PTL Club. They announced the donation on air. But Reba was homeless and living off the kindness of friends. She had a deep love for trees, plants, flowers, anything that landed in the dumpster at Walmart. She loved looking in their dumpster for what she could find. One day while I helped Jill's brother and father repair a drainage pipe in the driveway, Reba pulled up with trees she'd found in Walmart's dumpster. She had them tied down in the trunk of her car. To me, they looked more like sticks than trees.

She told Jill's father, "If you'll plant these in the yard, they will grow."

Reba's Trees

I laughed.

She cut her intense eyes at me.

I wanted to say, "Walmart gave up on them, so you can bet they are dead."

Jill's father didn't question her. He made me dig the holes in the yard. And Reba and I planted them and fertilized them.

Every morning, as the summer progressed, I'd look out the window at those sticks in the ground. I'd shake my head and laugh. One morning I noticed leaves on the sticks. They were becoming trees. Every new day produced more leaves. When fall came, the leaves changed color—bright red and orange. Out of all the beautiful colors on the trees that fall in Tennessee, none compared to the Walmart rejects. They were alive. Risen from sticks. Abiding in the soil of a new home. What the Savior has done was all there.

Mrs. Whitehurst called me into her bedroom one day and said, "Have you seen Reba's trees?"

I chuckled. "Yes, I've seen those sticks."

She said, "Have you seen them lately?"

I told her I had.

She said, "Never forget those trees, because a lot of times we look for people to produce spiritual fruit immediately, when in fact, it is a process that takes a lifetime."

Remission

1985

After the birth of our daughter, Jill's mother went into remission, and her father purchased a condominium and let us rent it from him at an affordable rate. It was just off the I-65 exit in Franklin. Not too far from where Jill worked at a salon.

Around this time, I answered an ad in the Lord's Chapel's Sunday bulletin. A church member was looking for painters. He trained me how to spray paint apartments. After someone moved out, we would go in and repaint the apartment, getting it ready for new tenants. I traveled all over Nashville in a baby blue Volkswagen Rabbit—that Jill's parents had given me—painting apartments. The man who owned the company would call me each morning with the name of the complex and the apartment number, and off I'd go. I'd drop Blair off at Jill's parent's house in the mornings and pick her up in the evenings. Mrs. Whitehurst and Blair became big buddies. She enjoyed being a grandmother. She picked Blair up from daycare each day and kept her in the afternoons until I could pick her up. I spent my day painting and listening to a Christian radio station out of Nashville that aired biblical teaching by various preachers. Furthering my Christian education.

Each afternoon, I'd sit and talk with Mrs. Whitehurst about life, the Bible, prayer, church. Just about anything. Her spiritual influence on my life was still strong.

But one day—her being an ex-English teacher—she asked, "Can I help you with your grammar."

I wasn't sure what she meant.

I said, "Grammar?"

She explained, and then each day the ex-English teacher corrected me when I used the wrong tense or used southern improper talk—*hissself; Done come over here for nothin'; I ain't goin do it; I can't find my keys nowhere.* Stuff like that. I'd say, "I done did it." She'd say, "It's just *I did it*. Leave the *done* out."

She would correct my grammar and teach me the Bible. Today, I still have a heavy southern accent and speak in broken English at times. But I'm better because of those afternoon sessions, where she convinced me that I was smarter than I realized. She believed I should get a college education, since I'd clearly not tried while in high school to learn.

She told me, "You could help troubled teenagers. So think about it. Plus, you should talk to Brother Moore about helping with the youth group at church."

I did both. I started helping with the youth group at the Lord's Chapel and entertained the wild idea of attending college. I wasn't sure what this meant, but I wanted to learn. Those afternoons with Jill's mother had awakened a desire for reading and learning, although my reading ability was slow and treacherous. I read every book she handed me. *The Cross and the Switchblade,* one of my favorites. I loved how gang members became Christians. I felt something of a kinsman with them. Not that I was that tough or rowdy. But it proved that people with rough backgrounds could find Christ and change their lives.

I applied to Middle Tennessee State University (MTSU) and sent my high school records. I had taken the ACT when I graduated. Back in my drug days. And I'd made a 12.

MTSU required me to take an entrance exam. Fifty people were in the room that day. I felt out of place, and almost turned around at the door. All the feelings of failure met me there. I pushed through them and sat down. I felt completely foolish for being there. I didn't know half the answers. I looked around as others worked with their heads down. Remedial classes in high school hadn't prepared me for that day. I knew college was out of my league.

Jill and her mother waited for my return home. I told them I didn't feel good about the test. Both reassured me and said I was always too hard on myself. I agreed.

Jill said, "You can always study and retake it."

The results came in the mail one day. I had been accepted on a conditional basis. I scored ridiculously low in writing, reading, and arithmetic. I couldn't speak correct English or write it. I could barely add and subtract. I read on a fourth-grade reading level. All of this meant I needed six semesters of remedial classes to get accepted into the psychology program, including Basic Reading I and II and Basic Math I and II. I was relegated to remedial classes and old feelings of stupidity resurfaced.

Mrs. Whitehurst told me, "Well, it's a high mountain to climb. I agree. But we shouldn't be surprised. It doesn't mean you are stupid, just undereducated."

It took Mrs. Whitehurst a month to rebuild my self-confidence, but I registered for class and started my eighteen-month journey to full acceptance, which started with simple addition, subtraction, and multiplication, working my way up to algebra. Basic writing classes meant lab hours where they taught me that "a lot" was two words, not one. I can still remember what the girl's face looked like that told me this. I felt shameful for being so dumb. To this day, I can remember shameful moments more than moments of success.

What Karen Horney said: *A person who eventually becomes neurotic has little chance to build up initial self-confidence because of the crushing experiences he has been subjected to.*

Mass-a-two-setts

1992

I took a full load at MTSU. Never missed a semester and kept painting apartments. I even took some classes during the summer. And six years later I graduated with a BS in Psychology. During this time, Jill and I had started helping with the youth group at the Lord's Chapel. Basically, just attending youth group on Wednesday night and chaperoning on youth retreats.

Things were good. Jill's clientele had grown, and we could pay the bills. We'd had another girl we named Sloan. We were still in love. We had survived an onslaught of our own mistakes. Then I dropped a bombshell on Jill and her mother. I told them the Lord was leading me to attend seminary. Neither one of them had a problem with me attending seminary, but they did object to where I wanted to attend seminary.

I'd recently met a man at a fast-food restaurant in Brentwood who quickly became a mentor. He rented a car and drove me to Gordon-Conwell Theological Seminary, just outside of Boston, Massachusetts. On the way, he taught me the correct pronunciation of Massachusetts. I pronounced it with a Tennessee twang: Mass-a-two-setts.

He'd say, "No, it's Mass-a-chew . . . chew-setts."

And I'd try again, unable to get the "chew" where it needed to be, while the rental car floated over hills and barreled through valleys.

. . . But before the drive to Boston, that summer, I'd met the man at a fast-food restaurant in Brentwood. Like I said, I was a painter then. My hair was long, my body skinny. Angular bones protruded from a shirt speckled with paint, only a few years away from a life of drugs. I was trying to figure out how to pray, so I hung out at the time with some veteran prayer warriors and listened to their prayers. They met every Friday morning to pray, then went for coffee afterwards at a Mrs. Winner's behind the boot store in Brentwood. God had delivered me, and I was trying to figure out how to pray. I was also trying to hear from God at these prayer meetings and thought God had given me a prophetic word for someone who doubted his love and guidance. I didn't tell the veteran prayer warriors because I felt it just might be my crazy imagination. Plus, what I heard from God scared me. God wanted me to tell someone at Mrs. Winner's this message: "God hears your prayers and he cares for you." That was it. He didn't say, "The person will be wearing a blue suit and red tie and eating a sausage biscuit." Yeah, I know. Crazy, right? What did God expect? Did he want me to visit each table and say, "I don't know if this message fits any of you, but . . . *he hears your prayers and he cares for you.*"

For weeks after hearing from God, I sat with the prayer warriors at the restaurant and watched people, wondering who I should approach with the prophetic word. But it was too scary to pull off, so I did nothing. I was shy. Not a good thing for God to give an introvert a message to deliver in public. Then a pattern emerged with a certain man. He was there each Friday like clockwork. I'd watch him eat, then leave the restaurant and hop in his two-seater Mercedes.

The following Friday morning, I decided to end the charade. When he went to exit the restaurant, I stepped in front of him and stuck out my bony hand with dried paint beneath my nails and said, "I'm Robbie Stofel."

"Roy Clarke, Rob," he said in a deep Bostonian accent.

I tried some humor in the awkward moment. "You're not the singer guy?"

He chuckled. "No, I can't play the guitar."

I smiled.

"Are you guys believers?" he said, pointing to the table where the prayer warriors sat.

I said, "Yes, why don't you join us at our table."

"I think I will," he said.

I knew he was the recipient of my prophetic word, but I still felt nervous about delivering it, thinking it may be a message from my own twisted mind.

Weeks elapsed. For five Fridays straight he sat with us at our usual table at the restaurant. And one day he told us what he'd previously thought was taking place with us—six businessmen and one painter who looked out of place among these white-collar professionals.

He said, "I thought you guys were counseling an addict back to health."

We laughed.

I said, "That's not far from the truth."

This exchange helped pave the way for my prophetic word.

One morning I finally got the nerve to tell him the message.

I said, "You know, I never told you why I introduced myself to you that morning. Now don't laugh at me, because I'm new at this Christianity thing. But I felt God had given me a message for you."

"Really," he said. "What's the message?"

"God wants you to know that he hears your prayers and he cares for you."

I thought he'd smile and say, "That's interesting," then move on to some other topic or conversation. So when his eyes welled with emotion, and he said, "The morning you introduced yourself to me, I was walking my block for exercise, telling God he must not be listening, that he must not care, that, I didn't even have a friend in this town. Then you introduced yourself to me."

Slight smiles were exchanged.

Then silence.

A few months later, Roy handed me a Gordon-Conwell Theological Seminary catalog and said, "Have you ever considered going to seminary?"

I laughed and said, "Never."

"I think you should consider going. God has his hand on you, and you need to think seriously about this. But the school is in Boston, and you would have to move."

I took the catalog and flipped through the pages, glancing up every now and then to see if he was kidding. I'd never lived out of the state of Tennessee. I'd visited the panhandle of Florida. I'd seen Rock City, but this meant a serious commitment.

I agreed to visit the school with him, so he rented the car and off we went.

When we arrived, we parked the car in front of an old church, got out, and looked in every direction, taking in the scenery of the campus. Inside the administrative building, I introduced myself with a long Southern drawl. They were expecting my visit, and they looked up from their desks and smiled and mused and listened intently to this Southern aberration.

I filled out an application, while Roy sat fidgety beside me. Then we nervously awaited their decision and paced the massive hallway. Thirty minutes later the jury was back. We clambered into the admissions office like father and son. I was accepted! No developmental classes, like MTSU. I mean really accepted! But Jill and her mother were not happy about my new aspirations, even though they respected God's calling.

Jill said, "Why can't you find a school in Nashville?"

Probably I should have, but it felt like God had a hand in it.

Freddy's Coming for You

1993

The plan was for me to move to Boston alone. I'd establish myself for the first semester. Find a job and get settled in, then Jill would join me. So we sold our house and moved back into the basement of the Whitehurst's house. Jill was supportive all the way.

In January of that year, friends helped me load up a U-Haul truck with our furniture, and I headed north to Boston.

One of the guys that lived across the hall from me in married housing told me about a job at UPS loading trucks on the graveyard shift. I took the job, and we rode together each night. Things were coming together for a great first semester, then I hurt my back and had to quit the UPS job. But I found a job at a psych hospital for teenage felons. My first day on the job, I walked up to the big metal door and rang the buzzer, and a man let me in. The first thing he said to me was, "If we have to gain control of one of the teenagers, you just grab an arm or a leg and hold on." That was my introduction and the extent of my job training. As I rounded the hallway, I heard hideous sounds and smelt this foul smell coming from one of the rooms in the hall.

Later, the man who met me at the door, took me to the room where I'd heard the weird sounds emitting and said, "It's your turn to do one-to-one."

One-to-one is where you watch someone and make sure that they don't hurt themselves or somebody else. He handed me a chair and said, "Go take a seat. Yell for me if you need me."

I thought, "Don't you worry, you'll be the first to know."

I took the chair, eased it down in front of the room, and looked inside. No furniture, just a mattress, just a teenage boy with his head hanging over the end of the mattress. I said nothing.

He caught a glimpse of me out of the corner of his eye and rolled his head to look me in the face. He stared for a moment then started banging his head on the tiled concrete floor and sang, "One, two, Freddy's coming for you. Three, four, better lock the door. Five, six, grab up your crucifix. Seven, eight, gonna stay up late. Nine, ten, you'll never sleep again."

Before too long, he became destructive to himself, and they shot him up with drugs and he collapsed into a man's arms. That place was nuts, and I never went back. Not knowing I'd work at another psych hospital for ten years in Alabama.

I was beginning to think my move to Boston was just as crazy. It snowed 86 inches that winter. Frigid blasts of Canadian wind got under my skin. I longed for spring and to see Jill.

Two months into my first semester, Jill called to tell me her mother's cancer had returned. Things didn't look good, so I quit school. We moved into the basement with no real plans except to spend time with her mother. We needed to be near and help, which was a blow to my whole supernatural-school-attending-scenario. Soon, I discovered that Gordon-Conwell had a satellite school in Charlotte, North Carolina where I could attend one weekend a month. I enrolled there and commuted 400 miles one way, once a month.

The last time I sat in the chair in Mrs. Whitehurst's schoolroom/bedroom, she said, in a weak and raspy voice, "I want you to know that I'm proud of you. You beat the odds." She paused and swallowed hard. "I know the move to Boston didn't go as you hoped, but Jill needed to be here, so thank you for returning."

My eyes welled with tears.

She continued. "You are my smartest child. And I want you to keep furthering your education. God has some great things in store for you. I tell people all the time how wonderful you write, and that you will become a writer one day, so keep writing. But, above all, be a good husband and father."

I nodded with tears running down my face.

Gone

1995

Jill's mother went from bad to worse and was hospitalized. She died within a week. I went to her bedroom and sat in the chair where she had taught me so many things about life and faith. My eyes drifted to the picture of the starving child in Africa that she had taped to the wall beside her bed to remind her that other people had it worse than she did. I got up and took the picture down, then I bawled.

My mother-figure was gone.

On the Road

1995

I'd been traveling to Gordon-Conwell in Charlotte, North Carolina for three years. One more class after the current semester and I'd be finished. To pass the time on the drive up to Charlotte, I listened to music and talk radio. And I'd made it a practice to stop at a Barnes and Noble store in Atlanta that was right off the interstate. I'd get a cup of coffee and walk around for a few minutes and stretch my legs. During one such stop, I was looking for something to listen to and ran across a book on compact disc called, *On the Road*. Read by Matt Dillon. I recognized Matt Dillon from the movie *The Outsiders*, but I didn't know anything about the book or Jack Kerouac, the author.

I had a hard time understanding the structure of the book. The plot seemed to be missing, but the cadences and the freedom it portrayed won me over. And I was blown away by the author's description. I'd give anything to write like that. But I hadn't written anything at that point, other than youth group sermons, which Mrs. Whitehurst had read. But listening to *On the Road* awakened my desire to write. Also, during this time I'd ran across a Southern writer, Larry Brown. I loved his gritty stories, which reminded me so much of my life growing up. I read where he was a firefighter that had never written much in his life, but one day he decided he was going to buy a typewriter and become a writer. He taught me about literary magazines. His story "92 Days" gave me a blow-by-blow account of how to submit to literary magazines, so I followed his lead. I started writing and submitting. Without much success. My mailbox was filling up with rejection letters as fast as I sent stories out. But I was learning. Then I had a story accepted at Austin Peay State University in their literary magazine, *Zone 3*.

Around this time, I was finishing up my graduate degree at Gordon-Conwell. Before heading to the seminary for class, I stopped in a Barnes and Noble store near the campus and stumbled across a copy of *Jesus' Son*. The title is what caught my eye, but I soon found out it had nothing to do with Jesus and everything to do with losers on drugs. I purchased it and stuck it in my bookbag and headed to school. Later that night in my hotel room, I read it all in one sitting. I didn't know you could write about losers, the lost, the damned with such tenderness and empathy. I finished the book and knew what I had to do. The following week I quit Gordon-Conwell again. I called the administration office to get the paperwork started, and my advisor couldn't understand why I would quit with only one class left until graduation. I gave some lame excuse, and I went and enrolled in the MFA program at Queens University of Charlotte. It's a low-residency model, so it already fit into what I was doing at Gordon-Conwell. I can remember sitting with two instructors, David Payne and, the poet and nonfiction writer, Jim McKean one night at an MFA campus party, and I had been hearing an unfamiliar term, so I decided to ask them what it meant. I said, "What is a trope?" They both looked at me like, *you've got to be kidding. How did you get in an MFA program?* But I guess they could see I wasn't joking. One of them told me what it meant. Now I feel shame telling you about it. But that's how stupid I was when it came to the craft of writing. But I kept submitting to literary magazines. Kept getting rejections in the mail. Over a ten-year period, I probably received a hundred rejection slips for every story I published, and I had published only a few. I also wrote three failed novels. Each one rejected. But I was consistent. I kept at it. Filing away the rejection slips and writing more stories and essays. Then I decided it was time to shop around a book of faith-based essays I'd written about living in the Whitehurst's basement. I submitted it to Christian agents and was shocked when I received a call from an agent at *Alive Communications*, one of the oldest and best agencies in the Christian market. They thought the book I'd titled *God, Are We There Yet?* had potential, and they wanted to shop it around. Some of the bigger houses passed on it, and I was getting discouraged. Then David C. Cook bought it.

Jill and I were elated.

Jill gave me a hug and said, "My mother would be so proud of you."

Music Therapy

2006

While working as a psych tech at the hospital in Alabama, I took the patients outside for a smoke break after lunch. And Jean, one of my favorite patients, wearing her usual pink fleece sweat suit, approached the desk that day where I was handing out cigarettes. We kept them locked away in the desk drawer.

"I need my tobacco," Jean said.

Her family had dropped off Bugler tobacco and a pack of rolling papers for her, not thinking about the fact that she couldn't roll. Maybe they couldn't afford real cigarettes.

I handed her the pouch of Bugler tobacco, along with the rolling papers. She took a seat at the table in the dayroom and rolled a cigarette while I let the other patients out onto the smoking porch. Her plump fingers struggled with the task. The final product was half-licked and loose, but I let her out.

"Don't pick the flowers," I told her.

It was my job to remind her. Administration had a zero-policy on pulling up the flowers on the smoking porch. Jean would uproot the flowers and put them in the outdoor ashtrays that have the capacity to hold 14,000 cigarette butts. These ash-buckets had a long neck that stemmed up from the base with two holes on each side, where smokers placed their cigarette butts, but Jean planted the uprooted flowers inside these holes or wore the flowers behind her ears. She was caught inside the revolving door of behavioral medicine and couldn't shake herself free of the place—being admitted and discharged at least three times a year. Her usual stay was two weeks to a month each time.

After telling her to stay away from the flowers, I took a seat in the dayroom where I could see the smoking porch through the unit window that ran the length of one wall in the dayroom. I watched her put the cigarette to the lighter on the wall and push the button. The lighter glowed cherry red and she took a few puffs. Then the cigarette broke apart and the fire tumbled out. She spiked the rest of the cigarette into the concrete and plopped down with her legs stretched out like a child throwing a temper tantrum. Her back against the wooden fence that surrounded the outer edges of the smoking area. Tears oozed from her eyes and spread into her wrinkled face.

Before I could get up and retrieve her, another patient in the dayroom pointed to her and said, "She's crying."

I put my key in the lock on the wall and opened the door. A cool April breeze swept by me and into the dayroom as I yelled, "Why are you crying?"

She yelled back, "Why didn't they buy me bought cigarettes?"

When she said it, everyone laughed, even the psychotics, and it hurt her feelings.

She screamed, "Don't make fun of me."

This was what made the place interesting and sad. I felt bad for her, so I used my old dope smoking skills—skills I hadn't used in twenty-six years. I turned her sorrow into an exhibition on how to roll a cigarette. The more I rolled the larger the crowd of patients grew around the desk. Everyone looked on in amazement. They asked, "Where did you learn to roll like that?"

I felt a sick sense of pride and kept rolling. The stack climbed higher, then I packed them into an empty cigarette pack, before handing them over to her. And Jean thanked me and started hanging out at the desk to talk with me. She whispered in my ear, "Joel Osteen is coming to pick me up, but don't tell anybody. I want it to be a surprise."

"It'll be a surprise all right," I said.

She smiled and said, "Joel Osteen and I are getting married."

"Isn't he already married?" I asked.

"No, that's just a front. His wife is really his sister. They just tell everybody they are married so women won't go clambering after Joel. He's got women all over him, but he's mine."

I never tried to persuade her otherwise. My day went better if I played along with hallucinations and fantasies. Then she said, "I have a fertile egg waiting on my man, Joel Osteen, and once he takes what is rightfully his, we'll have a daughter. We'll name her Jessica Silas Love. You know what Silas stands for?"

I said, "No, can't say that I do."

"It means heavenly body. My daughter will have a heavenly body."

She said it in such a sweet, syrupy voice that it made me wish the best for her.

She wasn't attractive. She had no teeth. She constantly wiped the drool out of the corners of her mouth with a rag she carried in the pocket of her pink hoodie. Her weight was unmanageable due to the meds. I wished she were beautiful for her sake. Abraham Lincoln said God must like common people because he made so many of them.

I heard Jean crying as I walked by her room. I found her in the bathroom, kneeling on a pillow in the bathroom floor, her body thrown over the toilet as if vomiting, but the toilet seat was shut, her hands clasped in front of her like a prayer.

"What's wrong?" I asked.

She said, "I know Joel Osteen is not coming. I know he'll never come get me."

I said, "Well, do you think you can live with that?"

"No," she said.

I said, "You may have to let him go."

"I can't do that. I can't live without him."

"Well, what if we let him go and not think about his coming for the rest of the day. Do you remember that song, 'One Day at a Time, Sweet Jesus?'"

I grabbed for sanity here. WWJD. What Would Joel Do?

"Yes," she said.

I began the song. Then she accompanied me, while I stood in the doorway of the bathroom and she remained bent over the toilet on her knees.

"One day at a time, sweet Jesus," we sang.

Then I said, "Come on. Get up. Let's sit and talk."

She stood, tears dripping off her chin. I helped her to the bed, then I sat in a chair beside the bed.

She said, "My first husband was a drunk, and my second husband sniffed glue."

I had no idea what to say, but finally I said, "Which one was the better husband?"

"Neither one." Then she laughed.

And I laughed, too.

She said her father abused her. Said she couldn't stop wondering why he would do this to a child. She said, "He did it to all of us." Then she randomly said, without the least bit of shame, "A cockroach crawled into my ear one night while I slept. It gives you a crazy feeling."

"I bet," I said.

"You want to know how I got it out?"

"How?"

"Peroxide," she said, "But it's not why I'm deaf in this ear." She grabbed her earlobe. "A raindrop infected it."

"A raindrop made you deaf in that ear?" I nodded toward the ear.

"Yep, a raindrop just dripped into my ear," she said, and the way she said it made me believe her, and it gave me a crazy feeling.

She said, "Do you believe in guardian angels."

"Maybe," I said.

"Do you believe angels can come to your bed at night and hold you?"

"It's possible," I said.

Who wouldn't want angelic beings tending to our sadness and loneliness?

The music therapist stuck her head in Jean's room and said to me, "It's time for music therapy. Could you round everybody up?"

One of the social workers was a musician and loved to play for them. It made for quite a show. Patients got happy. They sang and clapped their hands. And if the moon was in the seventh house and Jupiter was in line with Mars, they would dance. They would boogie.

I went room-to-room gathering the patients, calling out, "It's music therapy time."

I could hear the music therapist strumming his guitar in the dayroom. I looked back up the unit corridor to the dayroom and saw him bent over it, tuning it, trying to hear while everyone took their seats.

Once all had gathered, another therapist kicked things off by doing what the therapists called "checking-in." Like sailors taking depth soundings. This was the therapist's way of seeing if the patients were close to sanity.

The therapist doing the checking-in was battling cancer. At times she seemed lively, other times she looked tired. She was lively that day. Smiling, joking at times. She went around the group asking in a syrupy voice, "How are you doing today?"

Jean said, "Not good. My father died, my brother died, my sister died, my uncle shot himself in the head with a gun, and my children won't speak to me. And, today, my cigarette fell apart and everybody laughed." Then she started crying.

The therapist validated Jean's feelings. She allowed Jean to cry, to get it all out, offering her a moment of human understanding. It was hard to be a therapist to a bunch of psychotics. Making contact was the hard part. They didn't have appropriate emotions, so checking in could go in one of two directions. They could refuse to speak, or they talked nonsense with strange emotions, but I never thought Jean would praise my rolling abilities.

Jean pointed at me behind the desk and said, "He knows how to roll. He smoked marijuana."

The therapists looked over at me with quizzical faces. I'm sure what they thought of me didn't match that background. How

Music Therapy

could it? I was a pastor that worked at the psych hospital because my small church couldn't afford health insurance. I'd cut my mullet and thrown away my concert T-shirts almost three decades ago. Now I donned khakis and a button-down shirt.

My past was not something I shared with therapists. I have never been to AA or NA or received any kind of formal counseling for drug dependence. Mrs. Whitehurst had been my counselor. And my early years of faith in Christ were much like music therapy in a psych hospital. I'd found a church where walking through the doors leveled the playing field. The socio-economic lines blurred. Mental illness mingled with sanity, and this is always the recipe for a great church. Everyone is either a fool for Christ or an actual fool. And at the Lord's Chapel you couldn't tell the difference. At least I couldn't, and music therapy was like this.

After the therapists checked in with the patients, the music therapist asked if anyone had a request. Jean requested Johnny Cash's "Folsom Prison Blues." They sat quietly as the music therapist deepened his voice to a baritone growl.

Then another patient, who'd been having heart problems along with his mental illness, requested Kenny Rogers' "The Gambler." After group, he was scheduled at the main hospital for more tests. But for now, he sat in music therapy clapping along with the song and lip-synching the words, as if this song was taking him back to happier times, to a life that was simple and hopeful. I'd helped him take a shower before lunch. During the shower, he had a bout with uncontrollable laughter. He couldn't stop laughing. He laughed so hard he couldn't catch his breath at times. I envied him. I told the med nurse to give me what she'd given him. And when I asked him what he was laughing about, he said, "I wish you could hear these voices. They're telling the funniest jokes."

"Tell me what they are saying."

He said something about putting gravy over biscuits. It sounded random and unfunny. But maybe angels were entertaining him. Maybe they were coming to his bed at night and consoling him.

Once the music therapist finished "The Gambler" someone requested Elvis' "Teddy Bear," and the Elvis song livened things up. Jean and two other female patients stood and started dancing. Jean was a Go-Go dancer in a pink sweat suit. Her arms flaying the madness. The other two were doing nothing more than running in place while turning in circles. One was wearing sunglasses that covered half her face—huge suckers. She had on blue jeans with an elastic band, and she was giving the elastic band a workout. Then things took a chaotic turn. Jean started dancing wildly, flaying the air even harder, spinning faster—too much movement for this Elvis song. Then the song ended, and Jean hit the floor as if her intentions were to perform a break-dance move. She tried spinning on her back but scooted more than spun. Her dirty tennis shoes above her midsection like a half-dead bug. I tried not to laugh, so I started clapping. Thoroughly entertained. It was so tragic and hilarious. But I never laughed at them.

The therapist battling cancer helped Jean up from her botched break-dance move.

"We have time for one more," the music therapist said.

One of the women dancing with Jean requested "Danny's Song" by Kenny Loggins.

The music therapist looked down at his guitar and positioned his fingers. He began. When he got to the chorus, we all sang about not having money and about how in love we were, honey, about how everything was going to be all right. And in that moment, we all believed it. We were hopeful. It was on our faces. It was in our words. I even felt better. The only other place I've ever felt this kind of community was at the Lord's Chapel in those early days of my faith. All of us freaks doing the best we could to worship in our own ways—sweating, swaying, thought-blocking, listening to a charlatan tell us our hearts beat for a God we could not fully understand, praying in an unknown languages, hearing prophetic words from God, even if it was only the insanity of our own salience—gravy over biscuits, breakdancing in a pink sweat suit, sticks out of Walmart's dumpster, the beating of a heart for its maker. All great spirituality is about losing one's mind. It's like a

Music Therapy

calf reasoning itself to taking a bottle, when everything inside tells it not to. But it finds supplemental energy.

When the song ended, the music therapist strummed his guitar in a random way and said, "I enjoyed it. Hope you have a great day."

I announced a smoke break. Jean walked to the smoking-porch door, and I knew she would be okay out there. No more crying over a broken cigarette. I let her out and she smiled at me. We had each other's back. Everything was going to be okay.

What Richard Rohr said: *No one comes to God just by loving or suffering, yet only those who have loved and suffered seem to come to God more deeply.*[35]

Endnotes

1. Munk, *Arizona Sketches*, 65–66.
2. Armatage, *Cattle,* 33.
3. Munk, *Arizona Sketches,* 73.
4. Allen, *American Cattle*, 189.
5. Guzman. "Owning a Pet."
6. O'Connor, *Good Man Is Hard to Find,* 29.
7. Bowie, *When Christ Passes By*, 66.
8. Peck, *Different Drum,* 61.
9. Martin and Winer, "*Cioran*," para. 14.
10. Shields, *Reality Hunger,* 27.
11. Armatage, *Cattle,* 33.
12. Crews, *Gospel Singer*, 234–35.
13. Armatage, *Cattle,* 39.
14. Munk, *Arizona Sketches,* 61.
15. https://www.azquotes.com/quote/844701.
16. McCarthy, *Blood Meridian,* 130.
17. Bonhoeffer, *Creation and Fall*, 116.
18. Rohr, *Naked Now,* 51.

Endnotes

19. Allen, *American Cattle,* 46.
20. Watts, "Cows that Can Help Fight Climate Change."
21. Lamott, *Plan B,* 33–34.
22. Nouwen, *Essential Henri Nouwen,* 53.
23. May, *Addiction and Grace,* 59.
24. Armatage, *Cattle,* 135.
25. Peck, *Road Less Traveled,* 194.
26. Buttrick, *God, Pain, and Evil,* 134.
27. Nicoll, *Ten-Minute Sermons,* 55.
28. Shannon, *Hidden Ground of Love,* 297.
29. Merton, *Thoughts in Solitude,* 66–67.
30. Brown, *Billy Ray's Farm,* 67.
31. Jampolsky, *Love Is Letting Go of Fear,* 46.
32. Rohr, *Falling Upward,* 34.
33. Spurgeon, *All of Grace,* 6.
34. Buechner, *Going on Faith,* 52.
35. Rohr, *Naked Now,* 65.

Bibliography

Allen, Lewis F. *American Cattle*. New York: Taintor, 1868.
Armatage, George . *Cattle: Their Varieties and Management in Health and Disease*. London: Warne, no date.
Bonhoeffer, Dietrich. *Creation and Fall; Temptation: Two Biblical Studies*. New York: Simon & Schuster, 1997.
Bowie, Walter Russell. *When Christ Passes By*, New York: Harper, 1932.
Brown, Larry. *Billy Ray's Farm*, Chapel Hill, NC: Algonquin, 2001.
Buechner, Frederick. *Going on Faith*, New York: Marlowe, 1999.
Buttrick, George. *God, Pain, and Evil*, Nashville, Abingdon, 1966.
Crews, Harry. *The Gospel Singer*, New York: Harper & Row, 1968.
Zach Guzman. "Owning a Pet Can Cost You $42,000, or 7 Times as Much as You Expect." *CNBC*, April 2017. https://www.cnbc.com/2017/04/27/how-much-does-it-cost-to-own-a-dog-7-times-more-than-you-expect.html.
Jampolsky, Gerald. *Love Is Letting Go of Fear*, Berkeley: Celestial Arts, 2011.
Lamott, Anne. *Plan B: Further Thoughts on Faith*, New York: Riverhead, 2005.
McCarthy, Cormac. *Blood Meridian,* New York: Vintage, 1992.
May, Gerald. *Addiction and Grace,* San Francisco: HarperSanFrancisco, 1988.
Merton, Thomas. *Thoughts in Solitude*, New York: Farrar, Straus, & Giroux, 2000.
Munk, Joseph. *Arizona Sketches*, New York: Grafton, 1905.
Nicoll, William Robertson. *Ten-Minute Sermons*, London: Isbister, 1897.
Nouwen, Henri. *The Essential Henri Nouwen*, Boston: Shambhala, 2009.
O'Connor, Flannery. *A Good Man Is Hard to Find and Other Stories,* New York: Harcourt Brace Jovanovich, 1955.
Peck, M. Scott. *The Different Drum*, New York: Touchstone, 1988.
———. *The Road Less Traveled*. New York: Touchstone, 1978.
Rohr, Richard. *The Naked Now*, New York: Crossroad, 2009.
———. *Falling Upward*. San Francisco: Josey-Bass, 2011.
———. *The Naked Now*. New York: Crossroad, 2009.

BIBLIOGRAPHY

Shannon, William. *The Hidden Ground of Love: The Letters of Thomas Merton on Religious Experience and Social Concerns,* New York: Farrar, Straus, & Giroux, 1985.

Shields, David. *Reality Hunger,* New York: Vintage, 2011.

Spurgeon, Charles Haddon. *All of Grace,* Pasadena: Pilgrim, 1978.

Watts, Geoff. "The Cows that Can Help Fight Climate Change." *BBC,* August 2019. http://www.bbc.com/future/story/20190806-how-vaccines-could-fix-our-problem-with-cow-emissions.

www.ingramcontent.com/pod-product-compliance
Lightning Source LLC
Chambersburg PA
CBHW051101160426
43193CB00010B/1269